WITHDRAWN

MAN IN MOTION: *Faulkner's Trilogy*

man in
motion

Faulkner's Trilogy

W A R R E N B E C K

THE UNIVERSITY OF WISCONSIN PRESS

Madison 1961

Published by The University of Wisconsin Press,
430 Sterling Court, Madison 6, Wisconsin

Copyright © 1961 by the Regents of the
University of Wisconsin

Printed in the United States of America
by George Banta Company, Inc., Menasha, Wisconsin

Library of Congress Catalog Card Number 62–8085

To Marjorie
and
To James

acknowledgments

I acknowledge with deep appreciation the grant of a semester's leave of absence by President Douglas M. Knight and the Trustees of Lawrence College in the autumn of 1959, when this study was begun. For a part of that period I enjoyed the hospitality of Yaddo, whose gracious director, Mrs. Elizabeth Ames, I thank for that pleasant stay. At the home of my sister, Mrs. Marjorie Beck Lohman, I found another congenial haven for carrying on this writing. Miss Charlotte Kohler, long a kindly editor toward my fiction as well as my essays, gave the prompt reading which made possible the publication of some of this material, in an earlier form, as "Faulkner in *The Mansion*," in the Spring, 1960, issue of the *Virginia Quarterly Review*. During my absence from Lawrence College Professor Elizabeth Forter took on and, I am sure, enhanced my course in modern fiction. Mrs. Ruth Lesselyong efficiently and cheerfully saw to the copying out of my crabbed manuscript. My greatest debt is to my son, James Peter Beck, not only for close friendship during a trying time in my life, and for many a convivial dinner and much lively companionable talk, but for his constant and sustaining interest in the progress of this and all my work.

Warren Beck

Lawrence College
Appleton, Wisconsin
May 22, 1961

abbreviations used in the text

AA   *Absalom, Absalom!* (New York: Random House, 1936)

CS   *Collected Stories* (New York: Random House, [1950])

Dr. M   *Dr. Martino* (New York: H. Smith and R. Haas, 1934)

FU   *Faulkner in the University* (Charlottesville, Va.: The University of Virginia Press, 1959)

H   *The Hamlet* (New York: Random House, 1940)

ID   *Intruder in the Dust* (New York: Random House, 1948)

KG   *Knight's Gambit* (New York: Random House, 1949)

LA   *Light in August* (New York: H. Smith and R. Haas, 1932)

M   *The Mansion* (New York: Random House, 1959)

S   *Sanctuary* (New York: The Modern Library, 1932)

SF   *The Sound and the Fury* (New York: Jonathan Cape and Harrison Smith, 1929)

T   *The Town* (New York: Random House, 1957)

contents

MAN IN MOTION: *Faulkner's Trilogy*

1

_____

*"before itself, in advance of itself,
to have been at all"*

With the completion of the trilogy *Snopes,* William Faulkner has achieved a unique and imposing work of art, notable in a number of ways. Fully peopled, firmly inclusive of many and diverse events, it also represents a subtler reality, the complexity of experience itself. The trilogy's structure is freely elaborated, yet purposefully so; its intricate multiform design is progressively effective. The narration renders both dramatic and meditative variations on the theme of ubiquitous evil and its opposition. The causes and effects of that struggle are boldly delineated in their extremes by the grotesque not as incidental device but as a contouring and a coloration of the subject. The wheel of time, spun back and forth with masterly control, turns up facets of the truth, apprehensions the more intense for never being reduced to conventional definition, and forever struck across by the slanting light of irony. Ethical evaluation is constantly evoked, never imposed, as plot feeds more than

3

curiosity, implying that whatever the fate of individuals, for mankind the end is not yet, nor is the outcome assured. Finally, the richly detailed, momentous action, composed as an immense kaleidoscopic jumble which repeatedly falls into a new congruence, holds all together in a genuinely tragi-comic mode, opalescent, inviolable.

Twenty years ago, when with *The Hamlet* Faulkner had wound up his most creative decade, a so-called new humanist (discreet, not reconciled) could wonder aloud with genteel scorn whether there was anything of sweetness and light in this novelist's work. He required to be told that indeed Faulkner had a great deal to do with a sense for conduct. Others too had missed that point. An error, presently almost incredible, in much criticism of Faulkner up to and including *The Hamlet* was the charge of opportunistic sensation-alism, fundamentally nihilistic. It would always have been easier to prove that now and then Faulkner is obtrusively moralistic. More broadly, the basic strength of his work stems from a profound ethical concern.

This concern has had its roots in traditional concepts of human society and personality rather than in contemporary notions of socio-economic necessity read as inevitabilities. That perhaps explains why the extreme leftist literati, for all their assertiveness in the unhappy thirties, gave so wide a berth to the greatest American writer of their time, without acknowledging him as such. Seemingly by instinct they left him largely alone, as was their wont with all values not amenable to definition under the fixed terms of their ide-ology. It was certain conservatives, lacking vital experience of their own professed faith, who attacked Faulkner for being "immoral." Now those new humanists and their lan-guid followers, the plain professors of comfortable respecta-bility, are no longer heard, and now the alleged *enfant ter-*

rible of American fiction in the thirties has become the recognized old humanist.

And so another possible confusion looms, giving pause to anyone who would point out Faulkner's great sense for conduct. For the old humanist is also the old master. His strong ethical bent, obviously central in the conceiving of his fiction, is but the basis for it, not the accomplishment, the work of art. Yet it is only in terms of Faulkner's ethical themes that dramatic structure and aesthetic realization are to be fully apprehended in the novels. And in addition to this common but sometimes difficult requirement for the acceptance of the work of art as a total cultural product, there is a new and more special obstacle to the adequate reading of Faulkner, set up by a more recent sophistication, the distrust of sentiment itself, as well as of sentiments arising around value judgments and expressing themselves in idealistic attitude and conduct. Yet this is the point at which action and implication merge in all Faulkner's work, and it is out of this fusion that the work of art achieves its form.

All these factors, therefore, need to be considered *per se* and in their reciprocations for a full view of the trilogy *Snopes*. While some readers may feel that no one of its three parts is the equal, as a dynamic and composed work of art, of certain other Faulkner novels—most notably, perhaps, *Light in August* and *Absalom, Absalom!*—the trilogy as now discovered whole is in its way the very crown of Faulkner's creativity. To see it steadily also requires attention not just to its main narrative continuity and over-all design, but also to its intricate continuous counterpointing, those recurrences of detail which are never merely repetitious if considered from the altering angle of new context and with something of Faulkner's own willingness to take a second look for a possible refinement and enlargement of awareness. Indeed it is this process, both judicious and empathetic, and always avid in reconsideration, which becomes a central action of the work.

What the trilogy *Snopes* realizes, therefore, is the illumined sustained embodiment of an epically conceived legend, populous, circumstanced, and relevantly projected through all its intricate recapitulations and extensions. The creative vision gathers up its actors' retrospection, immediate experience, intent musings, and deeply intuitive apprehensions into the swirling nebula of the work of art, not just a continuum but the present as a presence, multiple-dimensioned, multirelevant. When Eula Varner Snopes leaves Faulkner's ethical protagonist, Gavin Stevens, presumably for the last time, he confronts some such realization, as he "heard the door and it was as if she had not been" and then corrects himself—

not that; not *not been,* but rather no more *is,* since *was* remains always and forever, inexplicable and immune, which is its grief . . . a dimension less, then a substance less, then the sound of a door and then, not *never been* but simply *no more is* since always and forever that *was* remains . . . . (*T,* 334)

It is thus too that Faulkner has comprehended his subject whole, orchestrating the fiction in resonances sounded on the great scale of ethical perspectives and humane empathies, with all the harvest or the curse of consequence, the burden or boon of contingency, known on the instant and by its memoried and peering light; and it is in this mode that the trilogy asks to be read.

Not for Gavin Stevens, and not for Faulkner, is man in motion so directly oriented as in Cummings' lines

> tomorrow is our permanent address
> and there they'll scarcely find us (if they do
> we'll move away still further: into now.

While Gavin might at least agree in principle that

> all ignorance toboggans into know
> and trudges up to ignorance again,

he would not see it as a continuity of simple successions. Instead, he thinks "it doesn't matter if they call your gray hairs premature because life itself is always premature which is why it aches and anguishes," concluding that "the tragedy of life is, it must be premature, inconclusive and inconcludable, in order to be life; it must be before itself, in advance of itself, to have been at all" (*T*, 317, 318).

In such a vision, committed to Gavin by his begetter, the past as a ghost, an omnipresent potential, is Elizabethan in its palpable commanding reappearances; left behind, it follows to stare in through the window from surrounding darkness; the past as exile comes home again, to complete the gathering in a present summary knowledge, and thus to prompt the continuously recurrent questions: what to do now, and where to go from here, and by what way, and for what reason, to what end—bespeaking man's constant fearful and desirous expectation, in that restlessness, this side of the grave, which is neither wholly his doom nor wholly his choice. The mood of this, the very experiential sense and feel of it, becomes the central thing in Faulkner, and the most contemporaneously pertinent, more so even than the massive sociological materials and the searching ethical inquiries, it being the psychological matrix supporting an ultimate dramatic reality, since only such a contextual rendering can reflect the human condition. Faulkner's work has always been basically and unequivocally humanistic, yet alert to the vagaries of men's consciousness and their variously directed energies, and magnificently ingenious in the devising of artistic techniques to represent this multiform, moving reality the more clearly in the scope of concept. The trilogy *Snopes* reveals at their height both the commitment to human verities and the range of realistic awareness, gathered up in a superb sweep of sheer creative power.

The eventful, intricate narrative comprises reactive moods of spectators and their interventions against Snopesism. Differentiated modes of the three volumes become complementary in a composed work of art. Faulkner's protagonists bespeak a humane view, yet individually, compounding complexity by idiosyncratic response. Flem Snopes as amoral aggressor is central to the trilogy, dramatically and thematically, by invariable opaqueness and intransigence contrasted to the concerned subjectivity and tentativeness of disinterested opponents. Stevens' championing of Linda is more than quixotic, as principled chivalrous response to moral challenge. The large-looming element of the grotesque, stemming from fictional conventions particularized by Faulkner's adaptations of style, also represents both the aggressor's deviation from the humane and the distortions produced by extreme resistance to aggression. Irony, as concomitant of the grotesque, becomes medium of the tragicomic, comprehending the contradictory involvements of human affairs. Thus Faulkner's conceptual power, humanely based, expressed in empathy and irony, renders the vision of life as motion, the continuum of being in transcendent human consciousness, immediately responsive, reverberant of past experience and projective of attitude and action, and thereby evocative of values, postulated relatively but with ethical relevance.

2

"if it aint complicated up enough it aint right"

Upstart Flem Snopes, the insidious small-time villain of *The Hamlet* who became banker in *The Town,* met his end in *The Mansion,* in retribution for his lack of fellow-feeling; the avenger Mink Snopes escaped, to move on through darkness toward his own place in the ground; Linda, Flem's daughter he never fathered, left Jefferson again and perhaps finally, after abetting Mink; and Gavin Stevens would seem to be temporarily out of avocational employment as witness and intervener in a world the Snopeses almost made. With the fine house emptied of a usurper who could never fully occupy it, the extended tale ends upon a pause, its implications suspended, as in the complementary reflections of Stevens and Ratliff:

"You see?" his uncle said. "It's hopeless. Even when you get rid of one Snopes, there's already another one behind you even before you can turn around."

"That's right," Ratliff said serenely. "As soon as you look, you see right away it aint nothing but jest another Snopes" (*M*, 349).

Once more a Faulknerian theme has been evolved, in an opulently detailed yet scrupulous fable of the human condition, with recurrent conflict between ruthless aggression and a principled resistance which is only partially successful, barely forestalling despair.

Ratliff's soothing "aint nothing but" echoes what he himself has been told by Bookwright in *The Hamlet* when the two men talk over a manifestation of Snopesism. Ratliff had predicted Flem would let Mink go to prison; Bookwright has wondered whether Ratliff's humane interventions included giving Henry Armstid back the five dollars, his wife's weaving money he paid for the spotted horse which injured him before it ran away. Ratliff, unsmiling now, speaks out against the total situation in total terms, mingling dismayed detachment and uncompromising conviction, while here it is Bookwright who does the bland reassuring. Says Ratliff:

"I might have if I could just been sho he would buy something this time that would sho enough kill him, like Mrs Littlejohn said. Besides, I wasn't protecting a Snopes from Snopeses; I wasn't even protecting a people from a Snopes. I was protecting something that wasn't even a people, that wasn't nothing but something that dont want nothing but to walk and feel the sun and wouldn't know how to hurt no man even if it would and wouldn't want to even if it could, just like I wouldn't stand by and see you steal a meat-bone from a dog. I never made them Snopeses and I never made the folks that cant wait to bare their backsides to them. I could do more, but I wont. I wont, I tell you!"

"All right," Bookwright said. "Hook your drag up; it aint nothing but a hill. I said it's all right" (367).

Over and over in the trilogy the action is to pause and turn upon such a point, facing both ways, acknowledging disgust and an imminent despair while reasserting an unsurrendered faith. Faulkner's spectator-interventionists—chiefly Gavin

Stevens and Ratliff, but including Charles Mallison and others —as protagonists of a humanistic ethic are very real human beings, both in their lonely falterings and in their recurrent resoluteness, and in any crises involving principle they are unequivocal, even when they, as Faulkner himself has admitted being (*FU*, 197), are "terrified" of the Snopeses.

There is, however, no oversimplified reduction to absolute extremes. *The Mansion*, like *The Hamlet* and *The Town*, continues to set forth involvement of relative good and evil in their qualifying interactions. In the elaboration of theme throughout the trilogy, complexity itself is a connoted subject, and its discovery is by glimpses and glances. Among the miscellany of characters is a criss-cross of overt stresses, but beyond that are the enigmas of motive. The obscuration of issue by devious behavior, the inroad of brute contrary fact upon theory, and the conflict of diverse claims are treated as aspects of reality, together with its complement, the clarification of issue as a primary human project, involving intellectual curiosity, moral responsibility, and determined action. In the represented lives there is still much misdirection or miscarriage, the centrally pathetic fact of waste is repeatedly touched upon, and the wrongdoers' lack of compunction saps confidence among resisters, who must face too the subjective trial of accepting distasteful means in a contest where the choice of weapons, as so often in reality, is made by the conscienceless. Yet in these confusions Faulkner himself is not lost, but maintains a dramatic and conceptual control, nor are his protagonists demoralized, however badly shaken. Their seriously motivated inquiries simplify issues sufficiently to allow direct intervention, and while much damage remains beyond redress, a fine sort of justice often gets done, although sometimes awkwardly.

And still the struggle continues. New difficulties aggregate in the wake of ameliorations; any advance necessitates defense of a sometimes more exposed position. Since the conflicts in the trilogy involve perennial questions of conduct, social and personal, campaigns may be concluded but not the war, it being the old endless one between light and darkness. Herein is the real complexity of all Faulkner's work, but especially of the Snopes saga as human tragicomedy. As to plot, Faulkner is doubly its master—its ingenious begetter and its firm employer for a subservient role. Certain eventualities round off episodes but there are no ersatz finalities synthesized out of melodrama or sentimental platitude. Instead the particular actions, however conclusive in themselves, are passages in an endless fluxion, and every survivor is still potentially in the running, since behavior is always joined to issue—issue as event and as value, and plot as more than spectacle, as stage for conduct and thus the frame of theme. To pause over the narrative's factual intricacies as the Faulkner problem is to be lost in multiple details which can be properly estimated only as to over-all concept realized in its ethical terms.

"Flem," the first of the four sections making up *The Hamlet*, sets the trilogy's course at once, with the arch-Snopes's acquisitive invasion of Frenchman's Bend, twenty miles from Jefferson, "Hill-cradled and remote" (*H*, 3), centering on old Will Varner's store, cotton gin, and a combination gristmill and blacksmith shop. Here Flem entrenches himself in a series of what become symbolic acts. To Jody's "You're Flem, aint you? I'm Varner," he only replies, "That so?" and spits (*H*, 25), as he often will; then with very few more words and none at all at the critical moment (*H*, 27), he insinuates himself into a job at the store. Soon Flem has risen to a position only technically second to the owner's and has donned a necktie—"a tiny machine-made black bow," the like of which he was to wear always, so that "it was told of him later, after he had become president of his Jefferson bank, that he had them made for him by the gross" (*H*, 66). In his first section Ratliff the itinerant sewing-machine salesman emerges too, as urbane opponent of Snopesism and an occasional victor in a struggle the outcome of which he says "aint been proved yet" (*H*, 31, 101).

Section two of *The Hamlet*, "Eula," deliberately told, centers upon the Varner's sixteenth child, the early-ripened indolent girl who, doing nothing, seems only to wait for the one not so far-off event commensurate with her abundant sexuality. Her allure becomes her fate. The mere sight of her is to infatuate many men but none equal to her, and when, pregnant by McCarron, she is conveniently married off to Flem, she is also bound over to the course of events which in *The Town* is to include her adulterous affair with the banker Manfred de Spain, her maternal anxiety over McCarron's daughter Linda Snopes, and suicide, all of which is to excite the amazed regard and compassionate concern of Gavin Stevens. The third section of *The Hamlet*, "The Long Summer," pairs disparate but complementary parts, involving perverse love and principled hatred. The first, containing the most highly rhetorized passages in the trilogy, concerns the idiot Ike Snopes's obsession with a cow; the second part shows Mink Snopes's murder of Houston after a lawsuit over strayed livestock, Mink's frantic efforts to conceal evidence of his crime, and his arrest. Thematically there is Ratliff's intervention to protect the idiot, especially from other Snopeses, and to aid the imprisoned Mink's wife and children; meanwhile the long-burning fuse of Mink's wrath against Flem is laid, to lead to the events, many years later, which conclude *The Mansion*.

The final section of *The Hamlet*, while it is a third-person recasting of the famous "Spotted Horses" story,[1] retains Ratliff as key witness and aloof wry commentator on Flem's exploitation of the community. In a sequel, however, the threads of irony are double-woven; Flem plants coins on the abandoned Old Frenchman's place, which Varner had handed over when Flem married Eula; and led on by the already injured Armstid, Bookwright and Ratliff (who would not buy one of the wild horses) are taken in by the hoax. To purchase the title to dig for buried treasure, Ratliff has traded Flem his share in a Jefferson restaurant, where Flem is to find his toe hold in the town. Thus still it "aint been proved yet" whether or not Snopesism can be contained; Ratliff has scored some points—notably in the goats deal, the profit from which he turned over to Mrs. Littlejohn for the idiot Ike's benefit (*H*, 100)—but Ratliff also has been caught off guard and proved vulnerable. Yet above all by holding his convictions against the adversary he has qualified for his role to come, as collaborator with Gavin Stevens, who is to take up the gauntlet against Snopes in *The Town* and *The Mansion*.

Throughout *The Hamlet*, varied only intermittently by bucolic humor, the dark note has persisted. Near the end of the book it resounds doubly, in two court cases. First it is heard from the Justice of the Peace, "'a small, neat, plump old man resembling a tender caricature of all grandfathers" (*H*, 369), who tries Mrs. Armstid's case against Snopes concerning her husband's injury by the wild horse, and who shows "amazement . . . bewilderment . . . something very like terror" (*H*, 370), then "bafflement . . . dread" (*H*, 371) and "pity and grief" (*H*, 372), until finally—like Ratliff under Bookwright's needling (*H*, 367) and like Hightower in *Light in August* (292)—he declares his personal verdict, "I cant

[1] *Scribner's Magazine*, LXXXIX (June, 1931), 585–97.

stand no more! I wont" (*H*, 380). At the conclusion of another trial Mink the convicted murderer struggles with three
bailiffs as he cries out to and against Flem, who, as Ratliff
had predicted, had not come to his kinsman's aid. But Flem,
in the last passage of the book, after a cool look at the victimized Armstid still digging and still enmeshed in the de-
ceit, spits over the wagon wheel and drives on, out of the
hamlet and toward the town.

For seventeen years *The Hamlet* stood alone, a finished
work of art done in four substantial panels, contained in its
rustic locale and bounded by its villain's arrival and departure. *The Town*, appearing in 1957, showed Flem in new
stances but at his old game, as the larger stage of Jefferson
not only allowed more ambitious schemes but enforced some
modification of tactics, while the man remained his unamenable two-dimensional self. Eula's appeal, and Linda's plight
in the grasp of Snopes, brought forward Gavin Stevens,
whose recurrent conflicts with Snopesism and quixotic devotion to its victims secondarily involved his nephew and
protégé, the more sardonic but not unempathetic Charles
Mallison. These two with Ratliff make up a trio who separately or in exchanges are varied chorus to the action
throughout *The Town*, even sometimes when they themselves are most decisively participant. What they regard and
estimate turns upon Flem's calculating tolerance of cuckoldry
which purchases him the economic support of Eula's lover;
what results is Eula's suicide, De Spain's relinquishment of
bank presidency and mansion to Flem, and Linda's liberation
from Jefferson, now that Flem no longer needs her as pawn.
Within the currents of these main events other Snopeses
appear, precipitating minor crises comic or melancholy, but
beyond plot, the central factor in *The Town* is the looming
presence of Gavin Stevens, in the representative ordeal of

his engagement as witness, devotee, interventionist, and elegist. Thus is laid the groundwood for *The Mansion,* with its gathering up of effects out of these intensely interactive causes.

Faulkner's note prefacing the terminal volume, and looking back over decades of work with the materials of the trilogy, admits "contradictions and discrepancies due to the fact that the author has learned, he believes, more about the human heart and its dilemma than he knew thirty-four years ago and is sure that, having lived with them that long time, he knows the characters of this chronicle better than he did then." Actually the discrepancies are minor and insignificant, and extensions of characterization do not disrupt earlier views but supplement them. If sometimes the reader's idea of a character or any detail in the action must be modified, this is made to resemble the way of actual experience, especially for the reflective, wherein with further acquaintance and a second thought another's deed or being is additionally seen into. This narrative process (so brilliantly practiced for instance in *Absalom, Absalom!* with its examination of Sutpen's rough massive figure from several angles and in differing lights) not only adds substance but amplifies aesthetic responses, deepening that sustained reciprocal play between the author's instances and the reader's alerted empathy. In this Faulkner is the completely modern fictionist and an amazingly masterful conjurer. He invites beholders into the world of a novel, to see for themselves and to experience discovery not just as information but as process, subject to revision and enlargement, and never resting in absolutes or in finalities, since Faulkner, with his acute sense of character progressively conditioned and society as operant and often fateful, knows well how what men do lives on both in them and after them.

Some of Faulkner's factual discrepancies come about from his ardent melting down of old material to a further and greater use—as when Cellini, casting his Perseus, threw in lesser stuff to make up sufficient metal. The substance of Mink Snopes in the trilogy derives from Ernest Cotton, of the story "The Hound," but it is much transmuted. Cotton is a bachelor, not a married man like Mink. Moreover, the strayed animal in dispute was a hog not a cow, and Houston's, Cotton being the one who wintered it and collected costs and an impounding fee from Houston; and the murder was less over the friction of that one incident than for Houston's arrogance, especially in the run he gave his savage hound. Beyond the reversal of these items when Cotton becomes Mink Snopes against Houston in the trilogy, what is chiefly added is the felt sense of life, set forth in a refinement of the transferred action, which is subordinated to the implications of character study. The resultant grotesque comprises in Mink a principled violence, a grimness, and a pathos revealed successively in several facets and developments from *The Hamlet* to *The Mansion*. Certainly in connected, self-sustained fictional works an artist may be allowed to modulate minor data (as long as the changes do not violate basic concept and are not distractingly obtrusive) in a transposition into another key. This is what is most typical in Faulkner's use of earlier episode—an extension and enhancement, in theme and evocation, as when the substance of the short story "Spotted Horses" was introduced into the fourth part of *The Hamlet,* but no longer as one of Ratliff's comic first-person yarns, and with the merged addition of darker tones which only a third-person narrative could comprise.

While Mink is progressively developed for the purposes of the trilogy, Flem's immediate family is reconstituted from earlier sources. Here the inherited tales, especially those going back to Civil War times, suggest some discrepancies, perhaps attributable to word-of-mouth transmission. The Ab Snopes who appears in *The Unvanquished* as horse-thief preying alike on Yankees and Confederates apparently was not invulnerable, Colonel Sartoris having shot him in the heel (*H*, 19) for trying to steal his riding stallion. But Gavin has it further that

the original Ab Snopes, the (depending on where you stand) patriot horse raider or simple horse thief . . . had been hanged (not by a Federal provost-marshal but by a Confederate one, the old story was) while a member of the cavalry command of old Colonel Sartoris, the real colonel, father of our present banker-honorary colonel. . . . (*T*, 41)

That being remembered, it excites "incredulity" when the Colonel carelessly takes a Byron Snopes into the bank, and it prompts the phrase, "the horse which at last came home to roost" (*T*, 42)—a view that is verified by Byron's absconding with bank funds (*T*, 119). Whatever may have happened to "the original Ab Snopes," there appears in the story "Barn Burning"[2] a limping man by that name, whose stiffened foot leaves a stain of horse-dung on Major de Spain's imported rug, starting the quarrel that ends in arson. This with its separate episodes condensed is reviewed by Ratliff in the first pages of *The Hamlet* (15–20), with reference to the Ab Snopes family just settled on Jody Varner's farm. In "Barn Burning" Ab had two sons, the elder "with muddy eyes and his steady inevitable tobacco" (*CS*, 20) and a younger, Colonel Sartoris Snopes, whose moral revulsion and reaction against his father's anarchistic outbreaks parallels Bayard's repudiation of hereditary code in "An Odor of Verbena"— and with something of the same racking conflict between

[2] *Harper's Magazine*, CLXXIX (June, 1939), 86–96; *Collected Stories*, pp. 3–25.

filial loyalty and responsibility to principle. Sarty, after warning Major de Spain, ran away, assuming his father had been shot. Ratliff remembers that besides "that big one, Flem they call him, there was another one too, a little one" (*H*, 15), no longer with them—"Maybe they forgot to tell him when to get outen the barn," Ratliff adds, in a fictionally proper ignorance of that boy's intense private experience so powerfully represented at the conclusion of the short story. Ratliff recalls too something not in the short story and contrary to its implications, that in a final altercation the morning after the fire, when Ab declares their contract canceled and is moving on, Major de Spain would like "to know for sho if it was you I was shooting at last night" (*H*, 20).

In *The Hamlet*, then, this notorious barnburner Ab, still a dour and compulsively quarrelsome fellow, has his primary importance as a factor in Flem's gambit to become clerk in Varner's store. He is remembered by Ratliff (*H*, 299) as among the kinfolk not any of whom came to see Mink in jail, he "moved into Frenchman's Bend to live with his son" (*T*, 5), there later, according to Ratliff, Varner noisily evicted him "from a house he hadn't paid no rent on in two years, which was the nearest thing to a cyclone Frenchman's Bend ever seen" (*M*, 123), and Ab is present, probably, in *The Town* as an old man of whom "Some folks said he was Mr Flem's father but some said he was just his uncle" (*T*, 129), though he never came closer to Jefferson "than that hill two miles out where you could jest barely see the water tank" (*M*, 152)—Flem's so-called monument and footprint after the brass scandal (*T*, 29, 73). Meanwhile the disappearance of Ab's younger son of "Barn Burning" leaves the stage to Flem, making more consistent Gavin's and Ratliff's view of the whole Snopes tribe as amoral, so that honest Eck Snopes, who loses his counterman's job for asking Flem what was in the hamburgers they were selling (*T*, 33), is a seeming exception who has to be explained by Gavin as one begot before his mother "married whatever Snopes was Eck's titular father" (*T*, 31), or as Montgomery Ward put it, the product of "some extracurricular night work" (*M*, 87).

Such a defense, which assumes it is better to be a bastard than a genuine Snopes, is not incredible to those who know them. As with the wild horses from Texas, their markings may vary but they are all refractory and in some way dangerous. As such in *The Hamlet* they become Ratliff's concern and reason enough for interventions. In *The Town* not only Gavin Stevens and Charles Mallison take on the problem, but others in the community sense the issue and offer incidental resistance, and thus Charles can explain, "So when I say 'we' and 'we thought' what I mean is Jefferson and what Jefferson thought" (3). As experiences multiply, Ratliff talks wryly of how they "used to laugh at them" (*T*, 44), and Stevens admits to himself that such jesting about Snopesism as "The horse which came home to roost" (*T*, 42) is really "Not witty, but rather an immediate unified irrevocably scornful front to what the word Snopes was to mean to us, and to all others" (*T*, 43). Throughout the trilogy Faulkner maintains a consistent view of them as a breed, but he does show mutations within it, especially with Mink and Montgomery Ward in *The Mansion*. When Gavin in *The Town* says, "They none of them seemed to bear any specific kinship to one another" (40), it paradoxically delineates them as a clan, by their common indifference to family ties. For advantage they will use each other coöperatively or cross each other, as may be most expedient. The range of such operations from the sordid to the farcical is suggested in *The Hamlet* (224–34) when the storekeeper Lump Snopes for his own profit allows yokel voyeurs to peep at the idiot Ike Snopes and the cow, and I. O. Snopes, spurred by Ratliff to do something about it to protect his current job as schoolmaster, uses specious argument and false arithmetic to make Eck bear the major cost. The two most differentiated Snopeses, Mink and Montgomery Ward, are individualized in terms of this issue of kinship. Mink makes his repeated appeals for Flem's help on that basis and considers it a monstrous dishonoring when they are not answered; Montgomery Ward, when forced by Flem to betray Mink or be abandoned to federal prosecution, is conscience-ridden and depressed by this double degradation of blood. Though Snopesism is a blunt and appalling cultural fact, the Snopeses are not seen as a brigade of identical robots. They are rather like pirates as conventionally envisaged—a motley crew, ununiformed, each wearing his personal anarchism with a difference, all of them destructive, but eccentrically so.

While Mink's obsession with his rights, Montgomery Ward's ambivalence between remorse and craftiness, and all other differentiations of Snopes behavior make for complexity, the reactions and actions of those other than Snopeses are even more involved, more variously revealed, and more progressively disclosed. Even in the consistently and objectively resolute Ratliff there are nuances; the elements are indeed mixed in the sophisticated and idealistic Gavin Stevens; irony shades the utterances of both men away from the primary colors of the absolute; the maturing attitudes of young Charles Mallison hang in an almost saturated solution. Eula Varner of *The Hamlet* is more of a Helen than the county can contain, much less understand, and in *The Town* her daughter Linda walks in a sort of silence even before her deafening and departs at the end of *The Mansion* in something of the same inscrutability that wrapped her in her girlhood. Some fictions attain consistency by a facile oversimplification; Faulkner has created in the opposite direction, with fidelity to his broad vision, and no allegation either of over-complexity or inconsistency should be entered against him merely because of demands he makes on attention and memory. Rather, a right reading must mark Faulkner's genius for manipulation of a subject matter large enough and veracious enough to represent a real complexity with all its lively conflicts, moiling confusions, and consequent pressure for resolutions which still can be only partial and tentative.

Certain charges of inconsistencies may prove nothing but the result of inaccurate reading, of the kind that has invalidated some journalistic reviews. An aspect of Faulkner's realism may operate here, in the simple form of discrepancies which proliferate when anecdotes are retold, especially if by folk with the common taste for evolving the well-embellished taller tale. A plain minor instance concerns I. O. Snopes in his phase as blundering blacksmith. Faulkner sets it down in *The Hamlet* that when Snopes "with the second blow of the hammer" drove a nail into the quick while trying to shoe Houston's stallion, he was "hurled, hammer and all, into the shrinking-tub by the plunging horse" (73). Later Ratliff, who had been away for a while, seems on his return to have heard a livelier version, for he mentions "That other one. I.O. That Jack Houston throwed into the water tub that day in the blacksmith shop" (*H*, 79). By the time Gavin Stevens is mulling over the case of I. O. Snopes in *The Town*, what he believes on hearsay is that after Snopes had quicked the stallion "with the first nail . . . Houston picked Snopes up and threw him hammer and all into the cooling tub . . . and led the horse outside and tied it and came back and threw Snopes back into the cooling tub again" (*T*, 37). Such amendings and outright revisions of Yoknapatawpha gossip are merely a multiple local color, the indigenous enhanced into the rich and strange.

A more prevalent, more significant source of inconsistencies is the fictional representation of individual points of view which may be in every sense partial. Since a basic Faulknerian device (and an effectively realistic one) is the discovery of the story through the speculation of bystanders, their specific statements must be seen in the dramatic context of whatever perception or misapprehension is theirs as of that moment. In *Absalom, Absalom!* there is not only the slow disclosure of "old unhappy far-off things" while Quentin unfolds what haunts him as legend and experience to the uninitiate Shreve at Harvard, there is also Miss Rosa's prejudiced portrait of Sutpen as demon—an understandable view from her point of disadvantage, but one which makes her an eccentric fictitious figure, not a reliable case historian. With Flem, comparably a focal personage in the trilogy, there is similar advance and partial penetration, but in an opposite direction. Sutpen, for all his crudity and ruthlessness, takes on stature and pathos in his pursuit of a more than material end, an ambition based in the establishment of family, and this is conveyed at intervals through channels as different as Grandfather Compson's observations relayed by Quentin's father or Shreve's amazed insights slowly dawning over his ignorance of the South and his lingering incredulity. Flem of *The Town* and *The Mansion* as viewed by the several thoughtful witnesses of his later career, repeatedly seems about to require a more charitable interpretation than *The Hamlet* allowed, and then as often forces recognition of his invariable meanness, in accumulations of increasingly damning evidence which nevertheless does not rule out possible reappraisal. If this is true of Flem, even more nearly a monolithic figure than Popeye of *Sanctuary*, still greater reconsiderations are stimulated concerning more complex characters. Their claims upon second thought prove no incompetence in Faulkner, but rather his responsibility to his subject, as to its interfusions and its comparative impenetrability. And since that subject is conveyed so largely through observers within the story, whose separate witnessings are both partial and progressive, any charge of inconsistency must wait on the saga's final events. In the review of evidence the discovery of contradictions will only prove how thoroughly the case has been gone into, as well as the limitations of any one character's vision. Beyond all that, of course, is the comparative incomprehensibility of life itself, to which Faulkner has been true, inquiring into the mysteries of personality and behavior with insistent curiosity yet with recognition of the enigmatic.

There are, of course, some sheer discrepancies of fact in Faulkner's work—though indeed considering the rapidity with which he has written and the range and detail of his matter, the wonder is that there are not more. What detractors have chiefly seized upon in the trilogy is the extrachronological appearance of his characters from first to last, by a manipulation of probable ages at certain points and an extension of life expectancy. Yet is Faulkner claiming more than a small fraction of a liberty resembling the compressions in dramaturgy's ideal time—by which in *Tamburlaine the Great,* after a hundred lines of exchanged threats and boasts between the protagonist and Bajazeth, twenty-three lines of back-chat between these rivals' consorts suffice for the completion of the great decisive battle off-stage. Marlowe does not keep his audience waiting while the sun declines and blood flows and hordes of men dispute miles of standing ground; Faulkner asks that Flem's longevity, the retardation of time's hand upon the otherwise beset Eula, and Gavin's fluctuant age be granted them that they may play out roles in a local pageant with a backdrop extending from the war between the states to that different civil war in Korea. Certainly Faulkner, in dealing with actualities beyond the actuarial, may be entitled to a degree of mythic scope, nothing so grand as that which allows Earwicker and family their historic reappearances, but proportionally as much increase as a buskin would furnish. The clock which by Cassius' count "hath stricken three" in Caesar's Rome sounds beyond an anachronism to tell most truly of a night not long enough for perfecting conspiracy, and of a near hour of reckoning. In literature there may be realities beyond the literal.

Faulkner's discrepancies, whether by rearrangement of things past or extensions of times present, should not trouble the responsive imagination that keeps not too far behind the artist's own. Within his invented fictional domain Faulkner has declared himself the "master of time," and since he feels his characters belong to him, he claims the right to "move them about in time" (*FU*, 29). The nature of the need justifies some arbitrariness in its fulfillment. This, in Aristotle's terms, is not a matter of history but of poetry. The characters have their being and live out their lives not in a rigid factual chronology but in the fluid continuum of a fable. Acclimated in the aesthetic-philosophic concept, "where transcendencies are more allowed," the actors become larger than life, and the progression is not just day unto day but through a modified and deepening knowledge, their own and their beholders'. And as to the broader critical estimate, these very discrepancies show how in spite of the vast range and interconnections of the whole Yoknapatawpha chronicle, Faulkner has been intent on the organic unity of each novel and with true creative purpose has made details stand about to suit the larger effect.

In the era of Flem Snopes's long progression from hamlet to mansion not only do familiar county folk reveal themselves further, sometimes surprisingly; the present brings past event into drastic reassessment, discovering behind the former overt action more of motive and mood. An extended view is bent strikingly upon Mink Snopes, twice a murderer, in young manhood and old age, briefly a tenant farmer and an almost lifelong convict, a formerly flat character emergent in the round, a primitive done with arresting detail. The opening chapter of *The Mansion* probes further Mink's ambushing of Houston after a quarrel over an impounded cow. In *The Hamlet,* where this killing was first narrated, Mink's elemental fury was singled out; and the brutality which drove his wife from him led Ratliff, in *The Town,* to pronounce Mink "out-and-out mean" (79). In *The Hamlet* psychological emphasis is on Houston's bitter aloofness after a stormy youth and the accidental death of his young wife; his is "that helpless rage at abstract circumstance which feeds on its own impotence," and he sees himself as "victim of a useless and elaborate practical joke at the hands of the prime maniacal Risibility" (215). Ratliff reëstimated Houston in *The Town* as "proud to begin with and then unhappy on top of that" and so "a little overbearing" (78). In his conceit, sorrow, rage, and compensatory arrogance Houston was both unamiable and pitiable, a typical victim of self under the stress of event, whose unease rebounds upon others. Now in *The Mansion* Mink's side of it is looked into, and in his more meagre pride and sorry efforts he is found pitiable too yet not without a certain dignity.

Any such "discrepancies" are "actively" (as Ratliff would say) an aspect of reality, being of the kind which may exist between a man's outward showing—the starkness of his wrongdoing or his folly—and the intricate conditioning of personality through which the explicit act was triggered. Such a variance is to be charged, if at all, to another creator than the fictionist, who has done his part when he brings to the commonplace event the revealing light of its private motive and cloaking mood, by which it becomes united in its very incoherencies with the whole history of "the human heart and its dilemma." Faulkner, moreover, deals forthrightly with incoherencies as such, for comprehensiveness and for that truth in depth which touches upon shifting relations of factors, the variables in the dramatic-thematic problem. His is not the easy realism of a so-called objective view which achieves its minor success by staying on the surface and never looking back; neither does he give inner action, the continuum of consciousness, without its generally contrasting frame of outward appearance, together with the impact of opposing event. The coexistence and interplay of the antithetical dramatizes "discrepancy" as reality, with all its appeal to curiosity and its challenge to judgment and compassion, and creates a consistency not as of exclusive abstract logic but as of the novel's world, aesthetically and thematically, and the world of men it therein shadows forth. Thus Houston, the tortured man of *The Hamlet,* turns under changing lights in *The Mansion* to become the simpler, more removed figure, while Mink's "meanness," seen into more closely, and literally reviewed in fuller relations, is seen beyond.

Mink is the underfed, overworked sharecropper with three bleak successes, two retaliatory murders and escape after the second. The murder of Houston is told of briefly in *The Hamlet* (250), where the greater emphasis is on Mink's disposal of the body and his arrest. Ratliff reviews the matter in *The Town* (78–82) as to Mink's expectation that Flem would aid him. Chapter One of *The Mansion*

(3–39) retells it all with fullest detail, colored by Mink's grim sense of provocation and his unrelenting purpose. A stunted little fellow (this touching detail is latterly given more emphasis), he lives by that endurance Faulkner finds in mankind, with a quietly courageous persistence making survival something more than a brute matter. He plays the game, too, according to dim but steady lights of his own. At first it is only one of the minute economic expedients of his marginal existence—he thinks to let his strayed cow stay and be wintered with Houston's herd and then claim it, fattened and perhaps bred, in the spring. When Houston charges for the cow's keep, Mink doggedly works it out digging postholes, but when Houston demands a dollar impounding fee, Mink does the added work and then shoots Houston from ambush, in an assertion of pride carried out almost ritualistically. On trial, Mink uttered the human claim for succor in elemental terms, as to blood, clan. His naïveté in supposing Flem would gratuitously come to anyone's aid lays him open to a traumatic disillusionment, and he goes to prison in the added bonds of an obsessive conviction that he must kill Flem when he gets out. But Flem has not only withheld assistance and communication; with typical craft he sees that Montgomery Ward Snopes, the purveyor of pornographic art, is framed for a lesser offense and put on shorter sentence into the same prison, and blackmails him (with threat of federal prosecution) to prompt Mink's futile attempt at escape, so that his sentence is extended. Mink's determination to be revenged is increased. He holds it through long years and achieves it at last against all that baffles an ignorant, almost penniless, and aged man, sustained by his code of vengeance and by his underdog philosophy that "Old Moster jest punishes; he dont play jokes" (*M*, 398, 403, 407). In motion, through time and circumstance, and under contemplation by other characters, Mink has emerged as something more than "out-and-out mean."

But *The Mansion* is not just a tale of the Flem-Mink opposition. A related element, more obliquely set forth but as important, is the role of Linda Snopes Kohl and Gavin's concern with her, which continues from *The Town,* becomes more than ever the business of Ratliff and Charles Mallison, and develops connections with Flem's whole story, his end, and Mink's agency in it. Linda's position in her home and her home town being anomalous (since Flem was not her real father and her mother had long been Manfred de Spain's mistress) and her experiences beyond Jefferson having been excruciating and injurious (sending her back from Spain's civil war a widow totally deafened), she reappears in *The Mansion* as one so impaired and isolated as to be awkwardly strange, pathetically incongruous. The summons to the chivalry of a Gavin Stevens is imperative. That his response often is quixotic illustrates him as man of feeling as well as aristocrat of the moral world; it also contributes to the drama, since his sometimes unusual actions are elicited by situations extreme in themselves, tending to force respondents into similarly strained postures and parries. Moreover, the Linda-Gavin relation, together with Gavin's precedent concern over Eula, is a focus of spectators' commentaries—those by Charles Mallison which in drawing on other witnesses from Charles's Cousin Gowan to V. K. Ratliff furnish the greater part of *The Town,* V. K.'s own halfdozen more succinct testifyings there, and several entries in *The Mansion* by these two as narrators of extended passages. Most importantly, the Flem-Mink confrontation and the Linda-Gavin-Eula involvement are not plot and subplot but that plot-paralleling, with essential thematic reciprocations, which is found in much of Faulkner's work—most notably in one way in *The Wild Palms* and in another in *Light in August.*

Skeletonized to its most striking incidents, *The Mansion* would seem a melodramatic climaxing of the trilogy—old Mink Snopes, pardoned after serving many years for killing Houston and for an attempted prison break, kills Flem Snopes (for ignoring and then betraying him) and does escape, with the connivance of Linda Snopes Kohl, the widowed, deafened daughter of Eula Varner by McCarron. These bare bones, however, as always in Faulkner's novels, are raised up fleshed with the pathos of personal ordeal, in conflicts magnified by ethical issue. Snopeses too numerous and Snopesism too insidious to ignore are observed and "meddled" with by the familiar trio, Gavin Stevens, V. K. Ratliff, and Charles Mallison. But though most of the main actors are the same and though *The Mansion* rounds out Flem's sordid history with recurrence to many events in the trilogy's preceding volumes and to earlier novels, like them it not only stands alone, it finds its pattern without any such conformity to a set trilogy-structure as was depended on by the authors of *U.S.A.* and *Studs Lonigan.* The narrative methods used in *The Mansion* sometimes resemble those of the first volume, *The Hamlet,* which was liberally omniscient, sometimes those of the second, *The Town,* where the narrating is all done in the first person, by Charles (ten chapters, 192 pages), by Gavin (eight chapters, 129 pages), and by Ratliff (six chapters, 28 pages). Tone is modulated too, from passage to passage of *The Mansion,* as it was in the preceding volumes. Faulkner's record stands, of never having written a novel for which he did not take a clean page, with his gifted intuition of the unique means that will best embody the newly projected material. It is this immense unflagging conceptual power, implemented by always readily tactical narrative techniques, which enables him to recapitulate, weaving the previously known into new contexts with the fresh and contributive variation of fine musical composition. Any of the three volumes of *Snopes* may be read separately, just as single movements of a symphony may be listened to, with satisfaction, but now that new readers (and they are to be envied) may take in the trilogy entire, its tremendous complexity and variety, held together not just by plot but by the thematic recurrence of modified detail, may seem more like a great opera. The three books not only complement but blend into each other. The omniscience of *The Hamlet* richly furnishes the stage and gives the narrative its tremendous impetus; the first-person reports which make up *The Town* turn illuminative speculation upon emergent facets of character and action; *The Mansion* emphasizes theme and resolution by apposing the two methods.

If to some eyes and ears *The Mansion* and *The Town* too may not seem Faulkner at the top of his bent, as variously manifested for instance in *Light in August, Absalom, Absalom!,* "An Odor of Verbena," *The Sound and the Fury,* or "The Bear," still the practice has not been reduced or muted, but merely specialized once more, with apt invention and strategic mastery. As a fictional structure *The Mansion* is typically Faulknerian, full of involved event, with a heterogeneous cast performing variations on main themes, in person or mirrored in others' speculative recounting. It is more broadly dramatized, with a greater variety of scene and actors, than *The Hamlet.* In its omniscient portions it attains a potency of imaginative realization beyond the levels of *The Town.* Yet it is a controlled plenty, neither wasteful nor irrelevant, and the narration for all its turning upon itself is steadily cumulative and—considering its intentions—even expeditious. Some criticism has charged Faulkner with a tendency like that which Ratliff (in *The Town*) attributed to the legal mind—"if it aint complicated up enough it aint right and so even if it works, you dont believe it" (296). But if tastes are not to be disputed, still they may be discriminated. A strictly rational temperament or one with cultivated regard for the classical as opposed to the romantic may genuinely dislike the complication, the fluent variation and incidental fullness, of Faulkner's narrative. An inattentive mind, or one which prefers conclusiveness on easy terms and the firm support of clichés, may reject Faulkner, even with self-defensive abuse of all his ways and works. Others, however, will accept this involuted fiction for what it is worth, in its commitment to complexity. Nor is this complexity a sheer subjective brooding either in the *personae* or by their creator; character and circumstance interplay dramatically, much complication is produced by aggression and corrective intervention, until, as Ratliff says, it is "all mixed up in the same luck and destiny and fate and hope until cant none of us tell where it stops and we begin" (*M*, 374). The method dramatizes a tentative approach toward relative certainties which do not preclude but rather make way for continued reëstimation. It accepts as a chief constant a recurrence in modifying context, where increasingly known familiar elements fall into successively new combinations and a return to the same finds identity of another aspect. This is how Faulkner "reads"—given responsive attention—and thus does the aesthetic experience reverberate in any faithful remembering. The effect resembles that of leitmotif, and as with such musical composition, in Faulkner's narratives recurrence is never simple, much less careless, repetition. New context provides the reference with fresh shadings and further distinctions, and if these are discriminated, no duplication will be charged, but there will be instead the sense of an extension and an enlargement.

Undeniably *The Mansion* is "complicated up," even more than *The Hamlet* or *The Town,* but the secondary developments are adjunctive to both theme and atmosphere, and they serve to extend an encompassing view of reality. Only as all this is discerned and credited as the artist's premise may his inclusions, procedures, and resolutions be fairly judged. Thus with Charles Mallison in Chapter Eight—before he describes the return of Linda from the war in Spain he takes a quick swipe at stay-at-homes who organize welcomes for returning veterans; then he shows how a personality can remain basically unmodified by superimposed experiences, in Tug Nightingale, whose father threw him out for joining the Yankee army in 1917, but who returned from France still believing as his Hard-Shell Baptist forebears had taught that the earth is flat; finally concerning veterans' returns Charles glances at young Bayard of *Sartoris,* who in trying to read the fate that had spared him and let his twin brother be shot down, sought to still his heightened natural Sartoris anguish by finding "just how many different ways he could risk breaking his neck" (*M*, 190). This last Faulkner had told before, but it comes in now as more than a garrulous repetition of Yoknapatawpha goings-on. For one thing, together with Tug's story, it suggests a heterogeneous though small community into which Linda is returning, where on different levels separate personalities show special attitudes too deeply rooted in heredity and early environment to be much altered by journeying a way around the world to war in a foreign land. Thus Linda does not enter onto a bare stage, and she comes as a stranger to those strange to each other and themselves.

Indeed, Faulkner's populous fictional backgrounds, so much more inclusive than traditional dramaturgy or "objective" fiction affords, rather resemble the cinema, glancing in this and that direction, showing life as crowded, with tendencies multiplying by interaction, and stress endemic. For pure entertainment the provision is bountiful, and many of Faulkner's subordinate episodes are among the heartiest humorous narratives in American literature. They never exist as interpolations, however. They are elaborations, but not extrinsic. Casually introduced, loquaciously extended, they still fall into place functionally in any reading attentive to theme and structure. "And one more thing," Charles calls it (*T*, 359), preëmpting the last dozen pages of *The Town* to narrate the incursion of four little "Snopes Indians or Indian Snopeses," sent as a tagged shipment from the fugitive Byron Snopes to Flem. It is rough-and-tumble comedy, the half-breed children breaking into the Coca-Cola bottling plant, their cooking and eating a pedigreed Pekinese (which cost Flem five hundred dollars in damages), their exile to Frenchman's Bend, where young Clarence Snopes was going to "train them to hunt in a pack" (368), and their almost successful attempt to burn Clarence at the stake (369), after which they are shipped back to Byron in El Paso. But it is more than slapstick; this extravaganza on the mingled motifs of Snopes aggression and aboriginal craft in living off the country becomes another episode in Flem's ridding Jefferson, for his own interest, of what Ratliff calls "Snopes out-and-out unvarnished behavior" (*T*, 370). Besides this immediate thematic relevance, the passage serves the aesthetic purpose of closing the novel diminuendo, a basic effect Faulkner has repeatedly shown mastery of, for instance at the conclusion of *Light in August*—the dramatic momentum and emotional tension of such a work making a reductive termination desirable, since it would be as abrupt to end with the penultimate Joe Christmas-Hightower chapters as to bring down the curtain on Hamlet's "The rest is silence." Similarly in *The Town* the four little Indians give a descent from the poignancy of Gavin's tears over the "terrible waste" of Eula's suicide and Ratliff's suggestion that she was "bored" (358), which Gavin has realized and elaborated.

Throughout the trilogy the subordinate episodes are generally comical, often broadly so. Such a tone is intermittent throughout the richly composed tragicomic spotted horses section in *The Hamlet*. In *The Town* the mule-in-the-yard incident is sheer hilarious uproar, which leads the old Negro beggar Aunt Het, an incidental participant, to remark afterward contentedly, "Gentlemen, hush. Aint we had a day" (256). But thematically the spotted horses auction highlights Flem's as yet completely unchecked and characteristically insidious operations, whereas in the business of the mule Flem must pay hard cash to extricate the disreputable I. O. Snopes and get him out of Jefferson, a proceeding in which Lawyer Stevens is asked to play a professional part. Compositionally the comic tone of the mule-in-the-yard episode corresponds with that of the discomfiting of Clarence Snopes by Ratliff in *The Mansion,* but this latter episode is reconstructed at second hand, with emphasis on the ironic, whereas the business with the mules is all-out fracas. In both, the writing is in the tradition of a precise and energetic regionalism, and within that localizing frame are seen the idiosyncrasies of characters very much on their own. However, Faulkner does not allow the minor episodes of his tale to fade out into sociological panorama peopled by supernumeraries scarcely more personalized than the silhouette-figures in statistical representations—as occurs at times in *U.S.A.* and *The Grapes of Wrath.* Faulkner's least seen actors are nevertheless real local folk, in a community where they are known to each other in a way, as well as not known. Nor do the eccentrics distort the picture unduly; while they are indigenous to the county and vine-ripened, it is also a bit of universally valid realism to show, through them, that home is where on any return you have to take it in, there being no place like it, just as those who remain must live with its involvements as more than novices and in less than complete comfort. Again as in the cinema, foreground is not drained but emphasized by depth, and the setting Charles provides by his glances in several directions is one which enhances Linda's role as well as giving it habitation.

In recalling Tug and Bayard, Charles is, however, more than a scene-setter, and he gets further into the act than as prologue in modern dress. Since he is one of the responsive temperaments through whom events are to be put into perspective (in this instance Linda's return and the impact on the town and on Gavin in particular) a general acquaintance with Charles's way of looking at things is relevant too. It is also presumably interesting *per se,* in line with Faulkner's apparent belief that anyone alive enough to get into a novel is worth reflective attention. Ratliff, in *The Town,* said all he "ever needed was jest something to look at, watch, providing of course it had people in it" (351–52), and while that is only the beginning, beyond which is response, it is the necessary beginning, humanly, and so of value in itself as well as a basis of judgment, empathy, and action. Thus the fictitious spectator, even without acting overtly, is part of the spectacle, and thereby Faulkner has approached an ultimate in narrative technique, the absorbing of medium into effect. The degree of this achievement is enough alone to put Faulkner into the front rank of novelists.

In the dramatic chorusing by Faulkner's spectator-interlocutors the problem of shaking down truth out of appearances is sometimes reduced to the simple difficulty of stating fact, within the limits of language and beyond the mists of rationalization. So Charles says, "Three weeks later I was back in Cambridge again, hoping, I mean trying, or maybe what I mean is I belonged to the class that would or anyway should, graduate next June" (*M*, 205). Such eddying fullness is one of Faulkner's most conspicuous departures from the contemporary norm of fictional style. Even in plainer aspects, where it is no more than an attempt to identify, differentiate, and define, as when Mink at the end of his trial is "hollering into, against, across the wall of little wan faces" (*M*, 3), it is sometimes criticized. However, it can scarcely be called turgidity by anyone who reads what it tells, whether the physical-psychological complex of Mink's appeal into-against-across his world or Charles's simple effort not merely to say but to see what he means, in an examination of his own probity before he scrutinizes the conduct of others, and not so much as a matter of conscience as to be practically sure no self-delusion is obscuring reality.

In his responses to complexity the spectator-character may also tend to an almost legalistic naming and fending off of contingencies—it is not this or even this, Faulkner's people say, but simply that—a practice which may seem to have rubbed off on them all from Lawyer Stevens (or is it *via* Faulkner from his friend Phil Stone, and will literary history some day have to cope with the theory that *he* wrote the novels?). Functionally this device of analytical narrowing down creates, within the total fictional illusion, the differing but converging dimensions of appearance and actuality. Sometimes the inquiry, while simple, has overtones of a search for subtler realization, as when in "Knight's Gambit" young Charles sees the perturbed Harriss girl in his uncle's office,

sitting huddled in the chair in a kind of cloud of white tulle and satin and the rich dark heavy sheen of little slain animals, looking not wan so much as delicate and fragile and not even fragile so much as cold, evanescent, like one of the stalked white early spring flowers (182).

More typically the successive discarding of approximations will probe beyond description for the definition of a subjective element, either as to the motive or mood of an action scrutinized or in the spectator-narrator's own feeling about it. When Flem withdraws his deposits and places them elsewhere, Gavin Stevens interprets it thus:

Not to destroy the bank itself, wreck it, bring it down about De Spain's ears like Samson's temple; but simply to move it still intact out from under De Spain. Because the bank stood for money . . . and as Ratliff said, he would never injure money (*T*, 278).

Faulkner himself, describing Houston in *The Hamlet's* omniscient style, distinguishes between reticence and preoccupation in this character's manner when

he would make one of the group on the gallery of Varner's store, talking a little, answering questions rather, about the West, not secret and reserved so much as apparently thinking in another tongue from that in which he listened and would presently have to answer (*H*, 245).

Imagery and state of mind are both touched upon with this analytic method in Faulkner's representation of Mink's children after his quarrel with their mother:

They were sitting on the floor in the corner, not crouched, not hiding, just sitting there in the dark as they had been sitting doubtless ever since he had watched them scuttle toward the house when he came out of the bottom, looking at him with that same quality which he himself possessed: not abject but just still, with an old tired wisdom (*H*, 254).

When young Charles Mallison, calling Gavin's attention to the adolescent Linda Snopes, remarked that she "walks like a pointer" (*T*, 131), Gavin noted it too, and "knew exactly what he meant" (*T*, 132), but saw also "the eyes not hard and fixed so much as intent, oblivious" and specialized the image further:

She went past us still walking, striding, like the young pointer bitch, the maiden bitch of course, the virgin bitch, immune now in virginity, not scorning the earth, spurning the earth, because she needed it to walk on in that immunity: just intent from earth and us too, not proud and not really oblivious: just immune in intensity and ignorance and innocence as the sleepwalker is for the moment immune from the anguishes and agonies of breath (*T*, 132).

Gavin carries on this definitive probing later to determine the basis on which he conducts his relationship with the schoolgirl Linda, as he feels that merely to speak aloud the words *reputation* and *good name* "would destroy the immunity of the very things they represented, leaving them not just vulnerable but already doomed" (*T*, 202), and adding that "innocence is innocent not because it rejects but because it accepts" (*T*, 203). It is with relation to this concept of innocence that he maintains for as long as possible Linda's illusion that Flem is really her father. Here and elsewhere Gavin is not splitting hairs, he is distinguishing principle by which to determine proper action in complicated circumstance, and it is in his passion to understand that he must be understood. While reputedly God is not mocked, man knows himself liable to be, and a real part of personal life is the apprehensive sniffing out and twisting of one's way past not only the deceptive, but the less true or even just the irrelevant. Fictional presentation of this process compounds curiosity, dramatizing the thrust toward truth in such speculators as Gavin, Ratliff, and Charles, and involving the reader in the action at its most intimate levels. Correspondingly the scrutinized character-in-action, whether a Snopes or Linda or a lesser figure, takes on deeper interest as to the alternatives he is presumed to have been capable of, his consequently acute experience of the problem of choice, and his self-revelation in making it.

This is only one aspect of Faulkner's fullness, but it is typical in substantiating a recurrent theme—the deviousness of much human motive, almost to the point of inscrutability, its frequently obsessive and aggressive nature, men's instinctive alertness against such possibly threatening qualities in others, and some men's instinctive sympathy as well with others' ordeals, extending to a partial understanding. To see all of Faulkner's elaborations in this light as a further sharpening and extension of fiction's basic concern with the character-motive-action equation is to find them masterfully composed. The strong underlying coherence in each of Faulkner's works exists in properly complementary terms: a sustained serious concern and a way of telling. This is fully the case in the *Snopes* trilogy, where the variations in narrative method, for all their extremes, are neither careless nor capricious but are brilliantly discovered ways to effect the dramatizing of concept. Faulkner is the genuine and constant as well as the uniquely gifted creative artist, whose performance is to be understood not by pseudo-classic criteria but according to his particular intention, and that intention, the mode of modern fiction, is expressed presentationally. The multiformity and miscellany inherent in his subject matter is comprised in an action, illuminated by imaginative attitude. Faulkner's fresh and effective realism, so close to fact through fidelity to the sense of fact, thus achieves the highest level of fictional art. Reality, though conceptually viewed, is never reduced to abstraction. The experiential is given aesthetic embodiment at once so dynamic and ordered that its complexity is the more revealed.

But if the tempi and tunes are primarily psychological, in movements of consciousness, the key is ethical. Curiosity, Faulkner shows, need not be idle, and its scrutiny may be extended to all phases of *what is* and *what goes on* with most serious reference not only to *how so* but to *what should be* or *should not be,* under the aspect of humanistic presuppositions. These always underlie the inquiries of the spectator-characters, and this intensifies drama not just when it prompts their well-meaning intervention but always as it moves them to private response of judgment and feeling, in lively processes as poignantly revealing as an Elizabethan soliloquy or a modern lyric. While these reactions may range from open anxiety to a cool irony, they always show a real involvement, primarily with immediate event and its participants but also with mankind, thereby suggesting that not only does one not need to send to know for whom the bell tolls nor attend the funeral to mourn, one need not be present in a court of law or summoned there in order to bear witness. Gavin Stevens', Ratliff's, or Charles's discourses and dialogues which carry sections of the narrative for pages will scarcely seem irrelevant or excessive animadversions to the reader who senses an ethical constant, not only in the character's rational observations but as his vital interest and hence the core of his dramatic being. It is this value above all which justifies Faulkner's inclusiveness, minuteness, and discursive method, and in its light Faulkner's scope will seem adequately contained in his art. Moreover, since Gavin, Ratliff, and Charles are all only human, as is fictionally proper, and since each in his attempt to understand and act rightly is limited and at times even frustrated by his own make-up as well as by circumstance, their enterprise takes on additionally an immemorial dramatic appeal, in finite man's confrontation of infinitely mysterious existence, with action as a constantly demanded response to specific issues in their emergence half-veiled out of a larger inscrutability and pregnant with consequence. That, it may be said more abruptly, is life; but indeed it is, and the full present impelling sense of it is the very breath of experience and hence of art, so that by their sustained representation of this reality Faulkner's works become, in the widest sense, classic.

3

"how to trust in God without depending on Him"

While there is a plenty, intricately deployed, in *The Mansion,* there is also an aesthetic gathering-up. It is nothing demonstrative, but a steady enlargement and enrichment through the varied weaving together of strands running back through the whole trilogy. They still disclose themselves further and with more crucial involvement in the prolonged sustained resolution composed of Flem's death, Linda's departure, the final acts and exit of Gavin and Ratliff as two old men still in motion, and Mink's turning toward the west and the kingdom of the dead. By alternating third-person omniscient narrative method, like that of *The Hamlet,* with extended first-person accounts like those which make up *The Town, The Mansion* achieves a wider range of tone than either of the preceding volumes, while echoing and fulfilling them, and treats episodes with greater discrimination of effect. Those readers to come whose fortune it will be to read the trilogy uninterruptedly and entire may find an effective aesthetic rounding out in this *a, b, a/b* structure, while beneath this is a more constant interplay and resemblance in that the omniscient narrative of *The Hamlet* is larded with lively sustained talk, while the first-person narrators of *The Town* are endowed with quite as much art as verisimilitude allows. *The Mansion* has three main sections: "Mink," "Linda," "Flem." In the first are five chapters, in the second six, and in the third seven. Eight of these eighteen chapters are first-person narratives, like those which made up *The Town*; the "Linda" (the second) section is entirely so, with V. K. Ratliff as reciter in the first two chapters, Charles Mallison (a man now, home from Harvard and the Air Force) in the third, fourth, and sixth chapters, and Gavin Stevens in the fifth. In the first section, "Mink," the third chapter is Ratliff's account and the fourth is by Montgomery Ward Snopes; the other three chapters in this first section, and all seven chapters of the last section, "Flem," are in third-person narration, of a kind generally corresponding to its use in *The Hamlet*. It is, however, a controlled and unobtrusive omniscience, wherein the characters still emerge as central intelligences, through whose particular views the story is unfolded and set into perspectives they personally apprehend. There is besides a special differentiation between those third-person chapters which center entirely in Mink (the first, second, and fifth of section one plus the first and sixth in section three) and the other third-person chapters, which make up the rest of section three. Each of these latter more broadly employs points of view of several characters and dramatizes these intelligences in dialogue which, as pronounced individual interpretation, approaches the effect of the purely first-person chapters. Finally, the five chapters (three in the first section, two in the third) all third-person, devoted to Mink's career —the murder of Houston, the long prison years, and the return to kill Flem—while tinged with his consciousness are nevertheless the most direct, conventionally controlled, and dramatic; all the others, whether first- or third-person, are more reflective, literally, or refractive—the event thrown back by some mirroring mind or focused through the lens of this or that temperament.

While Faulkner favors this essentially Jamesian-Conradian method, and has applied it variously, for instance, in *Absalom, Absalom!* and *As I Lay Dying,* there is another mode, quite as characteristic, in which his own voice is heard more personally, as style. Variously modulated, it pervaded *The Hamlet* from first to last. In *The Mansion* it comes out clearly in the chapters centered on Mink, yet moderately, under more than usual restraint. It resembles the parts of *Light in August* devoted to Joe Christmas, that other marginal and victimized figure driven to violence. There omniscient narration extends to a prose lyricism, which colors the account of Christmas's flight after his crime, especially in his morbidly heightened sense of his physical surroundings:

It was just dawn, daylight: that gray and lonely suspension filled with the peaceful and tentative waking of birds. The air, inbreathed, is like spring water. He breathes deep and slow, feeling with each breath himself diffuse in the neutral grayness, becoming one with loneliness and quiet that has never known fury or despair (*LA,* 313).

This is matched in Mink's consciousness, in kind. But not in intensity. Faulkner has kept the air of Mink's pitiful ignorance and naïveté even in the literate phrasings which elegize his predicament, and the style is always quick to return to the key and measure of the colloquial, as in the passage describing Mink's transfer to prison and his looking out from the train at

the Delta which he had never seen before—the vast flat alluvial swamp of cypress and gum and brake and thicket lurked with bear and deer and panthers and snakes, out of which man was still hewing savagely and violently the rich ragged fields in which cotton stalks grew ranker and taller than a man on a horse, he, Mink, sitting with his face glued to the window like a child (*M*, 47–48).

Mink's comment—"This here's all swamp," he said. "It dont look healthy"—evokes the deputy's cruelly ironic agreement, with the added remark that "a good unhealthy place ought to just suit you; you wont have to stay so long" (*M*, 48). Then as Faulkner continues, after naming *destination* and *doom*, he relinquishes the passage to Mink:

So that's how he saw Parchman, the penitentiary, his destination, doom, his life the Judge had said; for the rest of his life as
long as he lived. But the lawyer had told him different . . . and
even a lawyer a man couldn't trust could at least be trusted to
know his own business that he had even went to special law
school to be trained to know it (*M*, 48).

Recurrent variations in style in the first chapter of *The Mansion* are amalgamated into fluent but controlled repre- sentation of a complexity of situation and personalities. What "all Frenchman's Bend knew" about Houston is heard in their own idiom, as to his "sulking and sulling in his house all alone by himself since the stallion killed his wife," yet as the passage goes on, an adjective other than colloquial en- ters the description of his hound, "high-nosed and intolerant and surly as Houston himself" (10–11), but immediately thereafter, and with closer reference to Mink's own experi- ence, Houston is "a durn surly sullen son of a bitch" whose reckless riding would make a man "have to jump clean off the road" or be left "laying there in the ditch for the son-of-a- bitching hound to eat before Houston would even have re- ported it" (11). Passing beyond this predominantly colloquial tone, on the next page Faulkner employs a full style to represent Mink's intense mood as he waits for his cow, strayed into Houston's lot, to fatten and perhaps be bred,

cursing the fact that his very revenge and vengeance—what he himself believed to be simple justice and inalienable rights— could not be done at one stroke but instead must depend on the slow incrementation of feed converted to weight, plus the uncontrollable, even unpredictable, love mood of the cow and the long subsequent nine months of gestation; cursing his own condition that the only justice available to him must be this prolonged and passive one (12).

Despite its diction, the passage runs on the momentum of Mink's anger, and the polysyllables seem a multiplied and magnified but veritable echo of his cursings. That Faulkner is often elaborately rhetorical need not obscure his dramatic centering of the fiction in his characters' consciousness, acute under stress of issue.

In other passages in this same chapter Faulkner writes more simply while also more objectively, the omniscient author viewing his character from a distance that actually enhances compassion, as in the glimpse of Mink, when in Jefferson trying to get heavy shotgun shells for murdering Houston, waiting out the night in the railway station

—a small man anyway, fleshless, sleepless and more or less foodless too for going on twenty-two hours now, looking in the empty barren room beneath the single unshaded bulb as forlorn and defenseless as a child, a boy, in faded patched overalls and shirt, sockless in heavy worn iron-hard brogan shoes and a sweat-and-grease-stained black felt hat (36).

Faulkner's successive stylistic focusings are as various in range and treatment as are the movie camera's, and both his selection of detail and level of representation are determined by the aesthetic need and the opportunity of the moment, which he grasps with quick ingenuity. Such flexible rendering is more than the rampant virtuosity it is sometimes deprecatingly taken for. It serves a main purpose, contributing to thematic composition by its overtones. In the opening pages of *The Mansion* the multiple-phased picturing of Mink is not just an arresting narration in itself but a complement to what is to be the summary view of Flem as arrived occupant of the great house, where Mink is to come upon him at last.

In the third-person chapters other than those centered on Mink—and they make up the larger part of the final section —Faulkner expedites narration with succinct recounting and quick economical transitions, opening the way for dialogue which pauses contemplatively on the event. Thus in the main these chapters too employ the typical device of comment by dramatically secondary characters, functioning chiefly as witnesses engaged in that most serious human action of trying to understand and evaluate, but sometimes interveners also, in reaction to "the Snopes condition or dilemma" (*M*, 322), and especially to Linda's involvement therein as a nominal Snopes. Therefore a chief difference between these other third-person chapters and the first-person chapters is as between a one-man chorus in the latter or a consultative chorus, where with something like strophe and antistrophe Gavin Stevens and Ratliff or Charles Mallison, or sometimes all three, review and interpret the behavior of their fellows, including each other too. Faulkner's choruses, however, are not in the classic mode; they are more personalized dramatically, subordinating the voice of the poet, enfranchising the speaker as *persona*. Whether the comment is from any single character or in the dialogue of two or three, there are subtle but persistent stylistic variations to accord with different minds and temperaments.

In *The Mansion*, continuing from *The Town*, is another

sort of structurally related commentary, the placing of Gavin Stevens himself as a major dramatic figure in a thematically relevant role, by Ratliff and Charles, who recognize his high-mindedness and insight and also his intense nature and a consequent propensity to the quixotic. Even as a boy, in *The Town*, Charles had seen in his uncle

the eyes and the face that you never did quite know what they were going to say next except that when you heard it you realised it was always true, only a little cranksided that nobody else would have said it quite that way (*T*, 182).

Charles the Harvard graduate and Air Force veteran sharpens that view, but with no diminution of regard for Gavin's character:

Because he is a good man, wise too except for the occasions when he would aberrate, go momentarily haywire and take a wrong turn that even I could see was wrong, and then go hell-for-leather, with absolutely no deviation from logic and rationality from there on, until he wound us up in a mess of trouble or embarrassment that even I would have had sense enough to dodge. But he is a good man. Maybe I was wrong sometimes to trust and follow him but I never was wrong to love him (*M*, 230).

It is a rounded judgment which has been a long time growing, through the seasons of boyhood, youth, and manhood, and through vicissitude.

Heard by young Charles Mallison in "Knight's Gambit," Stevens' is "that bland immediate quick fantastic voice which lent not only a perspicacity but a sort of solid reasonableness" (179). Not every reader has detected the perspicacity, much less the reasonableness. They are there, however, and in such terms Gavin Stevens has gradually emerged as central member of the Yoknapatawpha world. In one important aspect he is perhaps its chief citizen, preëminent among judicious and compassionate spectator-interventionists, outranking even the remarkable Ratliff, and by good fortune sufficiently detached to be spared any such fatality of involvement as overtook Benbow, Hightower, or Quentin Compson. Stevens appeared decades ago, a young county attorney, as in the story "Smoke," where he is the shrewd courtroom lawyer and a detector of crime, a role he continued to play most intuitively. As district attorney in *Light in August* he becomes the speculative observer who, with informed sympathy and a transcendence of provincial prejudice, can imagine the compulsions in Joe Christmas from "that stain either on his white blood or his black blood, whichever you will" (424). In *Intruder in the Dust* by extended declaration as well as practical intervention he helps rear his nephew Charles Mallison to that moral maturity from which Charles in return observes Gavin and evokes him for the reader in "Knight's Gambit."

That evocation is continued in *The Town* and *The Mansion*, where Charles, further instructed by Harvard and the war, is now his uncle's colleague as a regarder of events and persons. While Charles's knowledge of Gavin is sustained and intimate, going back by family hearsay to Gavin's own young manhood, in *The Town*, it shows this most complex, perhaps most significant Faulkner character from but one side; it is a necessary counterpart to Gavin's involuted subjectivity, nevertheless, and a useful extension beyond Ratliff's common-sense observation, which shies away from Gavin's most extravagant imaginings. In all the representations of Gavin Stevens as philosophical commentator he has emerged besides as disinterested interventionist. Beyond this, in *The Town* and *The Mansion*, his involvement becomes acutely personal, as of one whose reflections must now take account of his own vagaries and indeed his own anguish. The factors remain complementary, however. What he burns through from first to last, in his emotional concern with Eula Varner Snopes and her daughter, Linda Snopes Kohl, is not only one man's empathetic concern but a confrontation of issues crucial in Faulkner's over-all view. Yet Gavin is more than mouthpiece. One of Faulkner's artistic achievements is the vitalizing of this rounded portrait shadowing forth the interaction of a highly developed personality and steadily accelerated circumstance. It eminently illustrates Faulkner's peculiar combination of boldness and subtlety, the surface done with broad strokes, the perspectives deep and delicately shaded.

A mitigating and indeed ingratiating trait of Gavin Stevens, even in his most fantastic moods and consequent quixotisms, is his fundamental magnanimity. Nowhere is this plainer than in Chapter Seventeen of *The Town,* devoted to his speculations about Flem's schemings during his vicepresidency of the bank. Gavin recognizes, with Ratliff, that Flem's basic aim is to be president, but he attributes to Flem sensibilities and value concepts transcending everything that the trilogy, through other more realistic eyes, shows about this most formidable of the Snopeses. For his part, Gavin supposes that when Flem had solicited Varner's vote for Manfred de Spain, his wife's lover, as president, Flem "not only affirmed the fact that simple baseless unguaranteed unguaranteeable trust between man and man was solvent, he defended the fact that it not only could endure: it must endure" in the interests of a "rectitude and sanctity" dependent upon "the will of man to trust and the capacity of man to be trusted" (*T*, 275, 276), so that in "sacrificing the sanctity of his home to the welfare of Jefferson, he immolated the chastity of his wife on the altar of mankind" (*T*, 276). This may be called a rash idealism, insufficiently examined as to the instance, and circling in the redundancies of its own dicta;

however, it also represents faithfully a typical error of the generous mind, the attribution of its own sensibilities and even its scruples to others. This can become, as it does with Stevens, the humane man's most dangerous vulnerability; yet its alternative, a complete defensive cynicism, must be worse, according to Faulkner's treatment of the question.

And as to the narrative, the reader need not be deceived by Gavin's too magnanimous interpretation of Flem. The more realistic Ratliff has never supposed that Flem viewed Eula's affair with Manfred as anything but a basis for advantageous deals, such as obtaining the light plant superintendency, and in the early pages of *The Town* (29) and again later (151) Ratliff has likened Flem's refraining from denouncing the lovers to the country boy's carrying a twenty-dollar gold piece pinned to his undershirt on his trip to the city, as a reserve for an ultimate need. For further guide to the reader, Gavin's wide speculations in the seventeenth chapter of *The Town* have been immediately preceded by Charles's account of Ratliff's more perceptive analysis, which while euphemistically indicating "respectability" as Flem's goal, plainly equates it with position; as Ratliff had put it, "Vice president of that bank aint enough any more. He's got to be president of it" (259). This simple aim for status measured as possession and power underlies all Flem's behavior, even his apparently affectionate leniency toward Linda, by which he induces her to make a preposterous will passing on to him her claims to Varner assets. What might seem generousness in Flem is found to be his playing upon the better feelings of others, not only an adolescent girl's wish to love and be loved by her supposed father, but Eula's concern that Linda have a name and at least the appearance of family, and old Varner's similar concern for both Eula and Linda.

All of which, however involved, is considerably more mundane than what Gavin postulated concerning Flem, a sacrifice to "the welfare of Jefferson" and the immolation of a wife's chastity "on the altar of mankind." Such extravagance leads to what Gavin imagined further, Flem's going out to Frenchman's Bend, to enlist the Varners against De Spain, in a surreptitiously hired car—"We would never know which one nor where: only that it would not bear Yoknapatawpha County license plates" (*T*, 292)—but then Ratliff tells him the plain and simple fact, "I taken him out there" (*T*, 295)—this done on his way to deliver a sewing machine. Even so, Gavin's most central speculations have been generally right, and often penetrating, with that gift of intuition which makes him sometimes the canny detective, sometimes the alert intervener in the nick of time, often the one who most understands the sorely beset. And perhaps, as is suggested in the fiction itself, as well as by Faulkner's regard for his own creative demon (*FU*, 204, 205), the price of such insights is the willingness to risk overshooting the mark now and then; perhaps too it is only with a magnanimity like Gavin Stevens' that intuition can be kept lively and empathy remain uncorroded by cynicism and despair.

Though Charles Mallison comments on Gavin's extravagances with a young man's humorous mockery, he perceives appreciatively his uncle's make-up. In "Knight's Gambit," where at the beginning Charles is "not quite eighteen yet" (139), he was already Gavin's protégé and companion at chess and conversation, welcome at the law office and permitted to hear everything that went on, together with his uncle's subsequent opinions. Looking back to tell the story of Gavin's eventful involvement with the Harrisses, Charles recalls "indeed a split personality," the evident "county attorney who walked and breathed and displaced air," and the

other the "voice so garrulous and facile that it seemed to
have no connection with reality at all and presently hearing
it was like listening not even to fiction but to literature"
(*KG*, 141). In other words, the youth, for all his easy use of
such terms as split personality and literature, does apprehend that his uncle's flights are not only beyond immediate
fact but beyond fictitious fancies into the realm of imagination, with its postulations toward truth. That the idiosyncratic
projection is not fruitless Charles begins to see, noting his
uncle as "glib, familiar, quick, incorrigibly garrulous, incorrigibly discursive, who had always something curiously
truthful yet always a little bizarre to say about almost anything that didn't really concern him" (*KG*, 165). Almost anything does concern Gavin; Charles really means things
which in the workaday way of life are none of Gavin's business or responsibility. But Gavin has in him something of
both fictionist and philosopher in his concern with conduct.
His scrutiny of motive is more than casual curiosity, since
his assessment of act and consequence is a step toward definition of values, their existence, accessibility, and cost.

Faulkner's agent in mythologizing the human condition
from the life of Yoknapatawpha County, Gavin takes on, like
any myth-maker seen close up, a peculiar appearance as he
studiously combines his disparate materials—local gossip and
representative verities. And Faulkner, in his attempt to equip
this complex and intensely concerned character, sometimes
may seem to draw the romancer's long bow. In "Smoke"
Lawyer Gavin Stevens is one "who could discuss Einstein
with college professors and who spent whole afternoons
among the squatting men against the walls of country stores,
talking to them in their idiom" (*Dr. M*, 136) and in *Light in
August* he appears "squatting among the overalls on the
porches of country stores for a whole summer afternoon" (420),

again talking the idiom, and this time there is reference to Stevens' Phi Beta Kappa key, which, while a less distinctive attainment than an understanding of Einstein, seemingly projects the same sort of adventitious glamour. Furthermore, Stevens has a Heidelberg doctorate, and at the conclusion of *The Mansion* he thinks of the purest of escapes into troubles all his own, by translating the Old Testament back into its "pristinity"—"its virgin's pristinity," in fact—an addiction he had been given to for twenty years at the time of "Knight's Gambit" (207). Considered as a sort of conventionally extravagant characterization, or storyteller's razzle-dazzle, this may appear regrettable, but even so, any such infrequent stain does not spread to the work as a whole, and at worst is no more than the sort of excess which occasionally disfigures the work of artists of immensely energetic creative force freely released. It could and perhaps should be viewed more appreciatively as a colorful stressing of Stevens the compulsive intellectual who is also and equally impelled to engage himself in the affairs of men, but always with intent to shape practice by principle, and so like other idealists he is prone to withdraw for a while to remote and higher ground from which to reclarify vision.

Nor is Faulkner the irresponsible romanticizer at large; he never confines any character within the formulae Charles found in his grandmother's library of novels from the '90's—

women who were always ladies and men who were always brave, moving in a sort of immortal moonlight without anguish and with no pain from birth without foulment to death without carrion, so that you too could weep with them without having to suffer or grieve, exult with them without having to conquer or triumph (*KG*, 143).

Even Faulkner's minor characters are particularized and give a sense of instantly and progressively reactive personality; as quick evocations they are as good as Conrad's lesser folk (which is saying a lot) and indeed they are done with something of the same firm economy and vividness. And Faulkner's major characters, like those of Conrad and James, are never the stereotypes of romance, whatever the range of the adventures and despite an occasional extravagance of gesture; they are rather epitomes of the personal displayed in aspects and in depth, considered as to behavior and as to conduct. The Gavin Stevens of Charles Mallison's judicious-affectionate view and of Gavin's own musings, confessional as well as inquiring, is a many-dimensioned, restless-minded, variously moody, and impulsively active fellow, and an adequate reading should grasp him entire and credit him in his sustained role. Otherwise the Snopes trilogy cannot be seen as an organic work, in which Gavin comes to the aid of that good man Ratliff and largely takes over, and indeed *The Town* would be rejected almost altogether (since Gavin's involvement with Eula and then Linda is so large a part of it) and only the Mink Snopes episodes of *The Mansion* could be fully valued.

Such exclusive criticism of the last volume has been made and may harden into another of the clichés which have hedged Faulkner about with impercipience. Objection, while a mode of criticism, should distinguish between mishap and malpractice, between a venial and a heinous offense, and just as Faulkner's lapses in syntax and diction should not be allowed to obscure, much less used to deny, his superlative achievements as a stylist, so Faulkner's alleged self-indulgence in dressing up a too charmingly quaint county attorney should not eclipse Stevens as key in the trilogy's design nor minimize Gavin as a very human being, in whom some oddities are the paradoxical outward sign of an inner vitality, and whose emotional responses and impulsive acts are complementary to rational insight. For such a man, living always at the top of his bent, life is both rewarding and tantalizing, and circumstance may prompt him to everything from portentous public diatribe to the most delicate scrupulosity in private relationship. The presenting of a Gavin Stevens requires a variety of shades and tones, and the brilliance and rich dramatic-thematic significance of Faulkner's rendition should not be unduly discounted because of what may be deemed an occasional exaggeration. Moreover, such allowance is especially to be accorded major writers, the great dynamic protean creators. Going full tilt, they risk some spills; and in their various ways Melville, Mark Twain, and James all overreach themselves at times, even as Shakespeare had done. Criticism must remain at least as proportionate as it would have artists be, and if it wishes any blotting of some lines, that should be without prejudice to many more and without neglecting a writer's achieved totality of expression and effect. Gavin Stevens is more than quaint, and what underlies his seeming eccentricities is really central to the trilogy.

One thing which especially shows him in a true and creditable light is his relation with the youth and young man through whose eyes so much of Gavin himself is reflected. The son of Gavin's twin sister, Charles Mallison grows from unofficial ward and hanger-on to be his uncle's established colleague in his extra-professional concerns. From his youth on Charles has never been treated as a simple apprentice, to be trained in the imitative practice of a method. Gavin instructs him on matters he is ignorant of, but also jests companionably with him, often confides, and always listens. He shows the humanist's faith that personality must be formed from within, that, as Yeats, in his philosophic prayer for his young daughter's wholesome maturation, puts it,

> The soul . . . is self-delighting
> Self-appeasing, self-affrighting,
> And that its own sweet will is heaven's will.

Gavin encourages such assumption of liberty and responsibility by the learner, and so while he admonishes if necessary, more often he merely directs attention implicatively. His most open instruction of Charles, near the conclusion of *Intruder in the Dust,* is in effect a confirmation of what Charles has learned independently, and is given with Gavin's profound person-to-person respect for that independence.

The trilogy has shown Stevens and Ratliff constantly learning, too, of course, but with specific additions to what they already know, and in the light of attitudes already consolidated, whereas in Charles a whole course of maturation has been traced, and from *The Town* into *The Mansion* that realistically fluctuant growth is still in process, though with no such crucial turning-point as that in *Intruder in the Dust.* There the boy Chick who starts to ride away from challenge forces himself back in acceptance of an imperative scarcely understood and indeed followed out in a sort of dream, although cannily too. It was an adolescent advance comparable to Huck Finn's, in that both boys were moved to put humane regard for a Negro above habitual deference to the mores of a regional culture, an excruciating reverse, the like of which is not seen in either Gavin Stevens or Ratliff. From the first in Faulkner's stories these two are formed men as to basic outlook; in Charles has been shown the making of such a man. This implies Faulkner's belief as observer of men that some of them, neither naïve, fanatical, nor eccentric, will not always pass by on the other side, but will accept engagement even in the midst of uncertainty, and will champion values disinterestedly, opposing not only preponderant conventions but harsh experience itself and the skepticisms it insinuates.

Such a morality must be personal; Charles Mallison does not become a copy of his uncle but evolves into quite as distinct an individual as either Gavin or Ratliff. In that progression, not only in "Knight's Gambit" but in the second and third volumes of the trilogy, Charles revises and extends his view of his uncle, and thereby too he enters into partnership. Besides setting forth central events of the trilogy in thematic perspectives, Faulkner's three chief witnesses, Gavin, Ratliff, and Charles, increasingly discover each other, and in those reactions reveal themselves further too. There is much interplay among such elements as Charles's maturing judgment and appreciation of Gavin, Charles's and Ratliff's comparison of notes on Gavin, Charles's private reflections on Ratliff's estimates of Gavin and dealings with him, Ratliff's independent easy scrutiny of his two more sophisticated friends, and Gavin's awareness of Ratliff's cool contemplation of his more impetuous gestures—all these given texture upon the strong extended threads of that ironic repartee by which these three in any combination show their reciprocal confidence and regard.

To make the grade into this club, through its members' acceptance and Faulkner's, is quite a thing. It is indeed the accolade for Charles that in *The Town* he is given so large a share in the reciting, for Faulkner spectator-narrators must be capable of a doubly manly commitment, meeting circumstance and facing issue. It is thereby that they so greatly enlarge and enrich the fiction. Involved in the event both as beholder and evaluator, the narrator becomes more genuinely the *persona,* and in the act of noticing and judging it is himself he tells of too, sometimes himself he celebrates, himself he mourns for. In Faulkner's technical scheme for pres-

entation of the trilogy, Charles as the third of such person-
ages, raised up by the patronage of Gavin Stevens and Ratliff, becomes not only autonomous but capable of contributing some unique points of view. An extendedly heard vigorous voice, a colorfully reactive temperament, a sometimes
advantageously removed spectator, Charles Mallison is a
potent factor in Faulkner's composition of *The Town* and
The Mansion. In parts of *The Town* he is even younger than
Chick of *Intruder in the Dust*; in *The Mansion* he is himself
as at the end of "Knight's Gambit" and beyond—Charles
Mallison of Harvard and the Air Force, come back to Jefferson not only as further learner and reviser of his more youthful views, but as seasoned young adult and increasingly
forceful spokesman. "Knight's Gambit," informative through
Charles's eyes and hearsay as to Gavin's early love for Melisandre and his late marriage to her after she is widowed, is
also notably the stage of Charles's emergence as young man
of the world, an assertive interlocutor, and a lively central
intelligence. While at the beginning he is "not quite eighteen" (*KG*, 139), at the end, in 1942, he is up to any give-and-
take with Uncle Gavin. His unfolding of events that center
factually on the Harriss family's involvement with the Ar-
gentine Captain Gualdres becomes basically a further look
into Gavin's mind, methods, and moods, but Charles's intuitions range in every direction. He sees the community's interest in Harriss affairs as betokening "what his uncle called
the spinster aunts who watched by hearsay and supposition"
(*KG*, 154), but he himself has inherited much of his knowledge similarly, "some of it direct from his grandmother by
means of childhood's simple inevitable listening" (*KG*, 143).
Carrying on from there, when young Charles first sees the
Harriss brother and sister burst in on Gavin, they become
"the puppets, the paper dolls; the situation, impasse, moral-

ity play, medicine show, whichever you liked best" (*KG*, 173). Thus has the objective-subjective dialogue begun to be the mode of his increasingly responsive existence, in which he is to assume his place as assertive colleague to his Uncle Gavin and Ratliff in their avocational brooding. That he takes to it not just as if apprenticed in the family business but in his own way, as the man he is and is becoming, shows once more Faulkner's sense and grasp of all that should be comprised in a dramatic action corresponding to the realities of existence, in terms of that responsiveness and accountable engagement which are measures of the humane.

It has a more particular flavor too, in certifying Charles's full-fledged membership in the guild of Faulkner's spectator-interlocutors, and attaining to their imaginative penetration of reality. In Charles's statement of alternatives, "the puppets, the paper dolls" of "the situation, impasse, morality play, medicine show," there is the typical analytic attempt to pinpoint actuality, together with an anxious envisaging of implications, fantastically expressed. The mode is basically poetic in that it is essentially precise and seriously concerned in its figurative voicing of intimation. Since with Charles too this extends so often to the grotesque, this may suggest to some that he has been misled, even corrupted, by his Uncle Gavin's example and Ratliff's; others may consider Charles's vigorously extravagant expressions a mark of his entry into full manhood, with its obligation of engagement and its prerogative of opinion personally voiced. In this a fancifulness even to the point of distortion, whether imagistic or conceptual, may be the paradoxical mark of a quest for the truth, pursued with insistent selectivity in the stress of a real concern.

Ratliff too falls into this mode of the fanciful. He has not learned it from Gavin or Charles; it was his way earlier in

The Hamlet, which he followed quite in his own fashion, no body's imitator, with accomplished tongue in cheek. It be comes at times a kind of parodying of his more educated and imaginative colleagues; it can also be self-satire for his bor rowings, by adding grotesqueness to extravagance. But Ratliff is no clown, and the most playful of his fancies tend toward the clarification of the immediate problem. Though wholly local fellow, he supplies some of the tale's larger per spectives as well as much of its precise data. And his natural aplomb is superb. He is the attentive friend (almost the courtier-jester to the titled man of law) who furnishes intel ligence of county affairs with canny analyses, brings a solac ing bottle to Gavin's office after Eula's funeral, and lends him a clean handkerchief after Linda's departure under dark implications as Mink's abetter. In the freer and more nearly equal relation of simple friendship, Ratliff is more detached and renders a cooler judgment of Gavin than Charles can. It nevertheless comprises extremes. At one point Ratliff re marks to Charles that Gavin married "would maybe be safe to live with then because he wouldn't have so much time for meddling" (*M*, 194), but while occasionally resorting to such humorous definition of Gavin's tendency (corresponding to Charles's "he dont want money: all he wants is just to med dle and change" [*M*, 196]), Ratliff also sees it as Gavin's "fate and doom" to have been born into an "envelope of boundless and hopeless aspiration" (*M*, 128). Intervention a sometimes the oddest of "meddling" for the soundest and most virtuous motives—this Ratliff can well understand, he being as capable of it and given to it as is Gavin.

Early in Flem Snopes's history, at word of his outrageous usury while Varner's storekeeper at Frenchman's Bend, Rat liff asked, "Aint none of you folks out there done nothing about it?" and when Tull asked, "What could we do?" Rat liff replied, "I believe I would think of something if I lived there" (*H*, 81). Later he does, entering in and acting decisively to shield the idiot Ike Snopes and civic decency in general (*H*, 225), and assisting Mink's needy wife and children (*H*, 297, 298). For seemingly even more gratuitous intervention, in *The Mansion* he is detected but not named by Stevens as the "anonymous meddler" (319) who turns the trick to keep Clarence Snopes from political office, by having boys brush the campaigning Clarence's trouser legs with damp switches from a thicket frequented by dogs, which follow through and drive Clarence from the rally, costing him the patronage of Uncle Billy Varner, who "aint going to have Beat Two and Frenchman's Bend represented nowhere by nobody that ere a son-a-bitching dog that happens by cant tell from a fence post" (*M*, 319).

In explaining what happened without openly admitting his part in it, Ratliff speaks first of "a kind of a hand of God" (*M*, 315) and then still more wryly of an "anonymous underhanded feller" (*M*, 317) who instigated the scheme; this is the more ironic in that Ratliff had moved against the deplorable Snopes politician only after incredulously asking Gavin, "You mean, even you cant think of nothing to do about it?" (*M*, 312). All this leads Charles to conclude that "what you need is to learn how to trust in God without depending on Him" and in fact "to fix things so He can depend on us for a while" (*M*, 321). In his uncle and in Ratliff Charles has repeatedly seen disinterested and sometimes necessarily drastic intervention as obedience to a moral imperative, in matters not always to be left to God, nor to some other fellow to be "a kind of a hand of God." Finally, in the complex texture of this episode, a bit of raucous folklore-in-the-making has evolved an ethic of "meddling" while illustrating Ratliff as sly and sober meddler, while canine habits together with a pious contribution to the prevalence of reason and the will of God have been comprised in one action; and the vulgar comedy of the method is enhanced not only by the worthiness of the achieved end but by Gavin's nice appreciation of Ratliff's humorous half-hintings as to how it happened. It is a typical communication between these two men so different yet so alike in principles and in faith that they can depend on each other's intuitions and relish an understanding all the more agreeable in that it need not be defined. And in Gavin and Ratliff there is a similar ambivalence; both men, like their creator, are quite humorous and very serious-minded. Beyond this, they are ideally complementary as dramatic figures and collaborating analysts. In Gavin the serious concern predominates, becoming tinged with melancholy, though never to the point of irresoluteness. In Ratliff humor is the most conspicuous aspect; his irony is something of a mask, almost as consistently worn as the neat faded blue shirt, but he is playful in earnest.

Ratliff's flow of wry jests and such comic tricks as that which discomfits Clarence Snopes as a politician are a veil for a purposeful engagement with reality, embracing humor inclusively, subordinating it to comprehensive intention. He shows too how the essentially philosophic mind can exist in the provincial. Not all of Ratliff's interventions are in the vein of practical joking either; what they have most in common is a dexterity the left hand is not permitted to know. In *The Town* he quietly supplies capital to save Wall's grocery business from Flem's financial pressure and attempt to dominate (148-49). In *The Hamlet,* after Mink is jailed for the murder of Houston, Ratliff arranges to have Mink's wife and two children stay at his sister's house, and he buys the children overcoats (279). Such plain philanthropy, however, is easy compared to what he has undertaken earlier concerning the idiot Ike Snopes and his addiction to the cow, which Lump Snopes is exploiting as a peep show. Ratliff looks too and feels a terrifying identification,

as though it were himself inside the stall with the cow, himself looking out of the blasted tongueless face at the row of faces watching him who had been given the wordless passions but not the specious words (*H*, 224).

Then he curses the men and himself among them, replaces the horizontal plank, and declares, "It's over. This here engagement is completed." To Mrs. Littlejohn he is able to explain something of what Faulkner calls his "baffled and aghast outrage" (226), admitting he is "a pharisee," admitting the cow is all the idiot has and that "it aint any of my business," and doggedly asserting a conviction he cannot verbalize but obscures when he tries to do so, saying, "I am stronger than him. Not righter. Not any better, maybe. But just stronger" (227). So Ratliff takes up the matter with the Snopeses, threatening I. O. with loss of his job if the clan lets the scandal continue, and the episode tapers off into double-edged farce as I. O. maneuvers Eck (who is no real Snopes) into paying the greater share for the cow that is to be slaughtered for beef to be fed to the idiot as a country cure for his perversion. Meanwhile Ratliff has stood by, has even intruded into the Snopes family council to see things through, though he has told Mrs. Littlejohn that "Maybe all I want is just to have been righteouser, so I can tell myself I done the right thing and my conscience is clear now and at least I can go to sleep tonight" (227).

Pragmatic in his operations, Ratliff still is basically principled, and when he cannot see his way he feels it. As the idiot Ike Snopes passes by, full-grown but dragging an improvised toy on a string, Ratliff remarks to Bookwright, "And yet they tell us we was all made in His image," but when Bookwright answers, "From some of the things I see here and there, maybe he was," Ratliff resists so dark a view, saying, "I dont know as I would believe that, even if I knowed it was true" (*H*, 93). In the same stoutly positive vein, in *The Town*, Ratliff says that "between what did happen and what ought to happened, I dont never have trouble picking ought" (*T*, 100). For all his wryness, Ratliff is as much an idealist as Stevens, and though he does not project abstractions as persistently as the intellectual is moved to do, he feels that a judicious preference may guide speculation, and thus he can suggest that perhaps "my conjecture is jest as good as yourn, maybe better" (*M*, 122). While this habit of postulation in terms of values joins Ratliff with Gavin Stevens, he is his own man too, and as a local unlettered fellow, widely traveled and acquainted in the county but not much beyond, he is the opposite of the learned man of law. He respects and admires his high-minded friend, but he is in no way overawed by the attorney as such. "Lawyer," he calls him,

a town-raised bachelor that was going to need a Master of Arts from Harvard and a Doctor of Philosophy from Heidelberg jest to stiffen him up to where he could cope with the natural normal Yoknapatawpha County folks that never wanted nothing except jest to break a few aggravating laws that was in their way or get a little free money outen the county treasury (*M*, 116).

Ratliff epitomizes a type Faulkner strongly believes in, the exceptional common man, unsophisticated but intelligent, responsible, principled, and plainly capable on a number of sectors. He is also quite as intuitive as Gavin Stevens; he surmises correctly that in her anxiety for her daughter's security and protection Eula had suggested Gavin marry Linda (*M*, 139), and he guesses Gavin's attempt to sustain young Linda's illusion that Flem is her father (*M*, 162). Ratliff's shrewdly realistic bent leads him to size up Flem more promptly and precisely than Gavin does, and he sees how in Flem's pursuit of "respectability" his "humility" is the practical kind which understands "they's a heap of things you dont know yet but if you jest got the patience to be humble and watchful long enough, especially keeping one eye on your back trail, you will" (*M*, 157). Even taken out of his environment and depth, Ratliff is still receptive and responsive, and in New York when the sculptor Kohl shows him his avant-garde work, Ratliff not only bears surprise without shock, he finds it a providence to "see and feel . . . what you never expected to and hadn't never even imagined until that moment" (*M*, 173). In his readiness Ratliff seems quietly equal to almost anything, with an unobtrusive assurance rooted in a calm rational integrity.

It is from such a vantage point that he exercises his ironies. They not only fall within a liberal tradition variously projected by Shakespeare, Swift, Jane Austen, George Eliot, Mark Twain, and E. M. Forster, but Ratliff more particularly belongs to a somewhat rare yet recognizably real American type, to be found as man in the street or the field or anywhere between in the common walks of life, the practical humorous critic of men and affairs, whose most casual remarks may be double-edged. The keenness is extreme, too; duplicity is met as such and penetrated by a superior device, in which *de facto* recognition of mischief is accorded so easily that it seems almost an acceptance, under which shield of appearance an uncompromising conviction strikes quick and true. And the duality of this method not only proves equal to that of the confronted situation but serves the mood of confrontation. As for himself, Ratliff could subscribe to what Conrad wrote of his own attitude, in preface

to *The Secret Agent,* that the sustained application of irony
therein was "with deliberation and in the earnest belief that
ironic treatment alone would enable me to say all I felt I
would have to say in scorn as well as in pity" (xiii). It is thus,
being paired with pity, that resistance to evil can make a
stand well this side of terror, in a genuine righteous wrath
held behind the mask of irony. Neither in panic nor for pro-
pitiation were the snaky-haired Erinyes renamed the gracious ones, Eumenides. The intelligent and honest Ratliff is
of necessity often worried and sometimes wrung by compassion, but he is never spooked. His rustic humor is more than
a yokel quaintness, his ironies are always conceptual and
usually satiric, being such a man's mode of intellectual and
aesthetic play, but basically an assertion of moral aloofness.
The further Ratliff spins it out, the plainer is the critical intent, as in the elaboration, delivered over the head of the
boy Gowan, describing Montgomery Ward Snopes in France
as Gavin Stevens' "hair shirt," and saying that the canteen
to which Montgomery Ward "added more and more enter-
taining ladies" was what would be thought

was just about the most solvent and economical and you might
say self-perpetuating kind he could a picked out, since, no matter
how much money you swap for ice cream and chocolate candy
and sody pop, even though the money still exists, that candy and
ice cream and sody pop dont any more because it has been con-
sumed and will cost some of that money to produce and replenish,
where in jest strict entertainment there aint no destructive con-
sumption at all that's got to be replenished at a definite produc-
tion labor cost: only a normal natural general overall deprecia-
tion which would have took place anyhow (*T,* 115).

Ratliff is not always so profuse; he is indeed more often
laconic, making his hearers guffaw or bringing any one of
them up short with a phrase. His wry wordiness can lead his

listeners, his succinct comments can open others' eyes, toward a realization of issue. It is the immediate and ordinary
that Ratliff deals with, but never in terms of the slipshod
conventions of a narrow community or the shrewder method
of men on the make. Ratliff himself in all this jostle is of the
saving remnant, a common man who is also civilized, being
both intelligent and intuitive enough to make some personal
claim as an heir of the ages, capable of value judgments,
committed to them, and blessed with consequent cheerful-
ness and poise. His subtleties (such as that deeply veiled hint
of how deplorable prostitution is in human terms) are in the
tradition of the parables; he knows that the truths he is concerned with must not just be heard but received with a personal assent, and he is quite aware of the hard fact that not
all ears are capable of hearing. Moreover, he shuns pretentiousness, and if he extends himself to the allusive, he dis-
claims all but a hearsay acquaintance with things cultural,
as when he calls himself "a interested party, being as I got
what the feller calls a theorem to prove" (*M*, 122).

Ratliff's and Charles's observations also serve to place
them, as in their confrontation of Snopesism they discover
each other's idiosyncrasies as well as Gavin's. Compared to
Charles and Gavin, Ratliff can take it slower and more equa-
bly because while he is the common man at his uncommon
best, perceptive and unfailingly humane, he is also the paro-
chial man, inured to the society he meets at its main level,
sound and able in the immediate issue, but without the
wider view born of education and its habit of abstraction,
except in those glimpses he half-humorously borrows from
Gavin, along with the erudite terms for them—what in *The
Town* (171) he called "old-timey" words. Charles Mallison
as product of university and military life, having the sophistication Ratliff lacks, is nevertheless still somewhat under

Gavin's tutelage, for instance as to the difference between *ashamed* and *sorry* (M, 110). Yet while Charles may often seem not only his uncle's disciple but understudy, he is a vigorous interlocutor in his own right, and here Faulkner, differentiating superbly, has caught too a younger generation's accent, the literate colloquial, pared down and toughened by self-defensive caution, more skeptical and less committed than his elders, but for that reason clearer-eyed in some situations.

Gavin Stevens in *The Mansion,* as in *The Town,* retains primary place, however, claiming it not in quantitative terms but largely as Faulkner's *alter ego.* He is a more controlled spokesman in the Snopes trilogy than he was in *Intruder in the Dust,* nor is he allowed in the concluding volume the broadly reflective lyricism of that passage toward the end of *The Town* in which he looks out and around from a ridge at night, seeing

Jefferson, the center, radiating weakly its puny glow into space; beyond it . . . the County, tied by the diverging roads to that center . . . yourself detached . . . above the cradle of your nativity . . . the record and chronicle of your native land proffered for your perusal in ring by concentric ring like the ripples on living water above the dreamless slumber of your past,

and so on (315–16). Gavin Stevens is still that man, however, reflectively observant and compassionate, as Faulkner the novelist is forever that sort of man, paradoxically the more involved because of detachment and its perspective, since the artist, like the saint, is allowed his visions only under a charge of complete accountability to them. Gavin, with quite as much human imperfection and eccentricity as some of the great saints, is also, like them, capable of intense sustained devotion, and indeed cannot resist the impulse to commitment. So, unlike Teufelsdröckh, he must come down from his height of outlook and enter the strife. Commentator concerning the human situation under the aspect of humanistic assumptions, and also the interventionist on principle, by his generous sentiments he is made vulnerable to severe private ordeal. Yet while Faulkner's primary spokesman is actor as well, and the chief voice as chorus is also at times protagonist, there is no thematic or aesthetic disunity in that, since both commentary and intervention are responses to situation, and have been reciprocally evolved in it.

The technique of first-person narrative which in Faulkner's three main interlocutors is focused chiefly on Snopesism has a significant extension in *The Mansion*, in that a Snopes, Montgomery Ward, is allowed to tell his own story and to ponder his involvement with Flem and Mink. Montgomery Ward, who having added prostitution to the wartime Y.M.C.A.'s services in France, had brough French pornography to Yoknapatawpha County in his Atelier Monty, now wins the privilege of testifying by rising to a degree of conscience and compassion—though neither is strong enough to reform him but merely to trouble him. The compassion appears in his view of Miss Reba, the ageing Memphis madam, with

"the fat raddled face and body that had worn themselves out with the simple hard physical work of being a whore and making a living at it like an old prize fighter or football player . . . and the eyes with something in or behind them that shouldn't have been there; that, as they say, shouldn't happen to a dog" (*M*, 79).

To Miss Reba he entrusts (*M*, 82) forty dollars of the money Flem has provided for a Memphis debauch and asks her to send it anonymously to Mink in prison, where he is about to join him, on a trumped-up charge, to implement Flem's betrayal of Mink. Conscience punishes him as he tricks Mink into the attempted prison break which gets his sentence extended and protects Flem from his vengeance that much longer. Flem having forced Montgomery Ward's connivance only by threatening exposure to federal prosecution, Montgomery Ward "had to watch it too," and with something beyond a Snopes's amoral egoism he sees the deceived Mink, starting out to escape in the provided calico dress and sunbonnet disguise, walking "as forlorn and lonely and fragile and alien . . . as a paper doll blowing across a rolling mill" (*M*, 85).

So when Montgomery Ward counts himself "just another Snopes son of a bitch" (*M*, 87), he is minimizing both the good and the bad in himself, practicing modernity's secularizing of the proposition that we are all miserable sinners, to furnish everyman a fatalistic do-it-yourself absolution, with no more comfortable words than what the hell. Actually Faulkner has made Montgomery Ward quite different from both Mink and Flem. Whether better or worse than Mink may depend partly on what ratio is given perception and responsibility, but Faulkner does not dally with such tangential abstractions; he keeps ethical issues centered and dramatized in his characters' being, responses, and anguish in regard to situation. And Montgomery Ward is not too unlike many other Faulkner characters (or many a man) in his unhappy combination of sensitivity and harshness; the striking thing is that in *The Mansion* he acquires a voice *in propria persona* and undertakes an assessment of events and behavior, the only Snopes given such a direct hearing. This extreme instance from Faulkner's practice has primarily a quite sound thematic and structural function, but it shows also Faulkner's ceaseless interest in character-action, action-character as the reversible equation basic to fiction. Furthermore, it displays his passion for figuring most minutely the personalities of his actors, exploring subtlest and perhaps generally unrecognized conditionings of behavior, with resultant shifts for the reader in the shadings of the dramatic action itself.

Finally, in Montgomery Ward's self-accusation, "just another Snopes son of a bitch," he not only bespeaks a morbid sense of clan as predestination, but by the stock expletive he unconsciously sets up an ironic connection with a larger theme that echoes through *The Mansion*. Miss Reba, on hearing of Houston's murder, had asked if he deserved it, and being told that at least "he sure worked to earn it," says, "The poor son of a bitch." Then when she takes Montgomery Ward's forty dollars to send to Mink, she repeats the phrase, and being asked whether now she is talking about the murdered man or his murderer, replies, "Both of them. All of us. Every one of us. The poor son of a bitches" (*M*, 82), and in her curious syntax men and women have become mankind, and the pathos of the human condition has been adduced. Goodyhay, the fanatic ex-Marine preacher, repeatedly prays in the same idiom, "Save us, Christ, the poor sons of bitches" (*M*, 271, 282). Ratliff and Stevens use the phrase in a kind of antiphon, following Stevens' pronouncement that "People just do the best they can" (*M*, 429). Ratliff, suggesting that maybe Flem, like Eula, "was jest bored too," adds, "The pore son of a bitch," and Stevens, explaining that Flem was impotent, generalizes it again, as to "The poor sons of bitches that have to cause all the grief and anguish they have to cause!" (*M*, 430).

In every case the vulgar phrase projects a reflective estimate of others, with that degree if not of identification at least of humane recognition which merges judgment and compassion as may be. The scrutiny of conduct, represented as a basic reality because it is an acceptance of personal involvement with mankind, becomes the source of action and a central action in itself, "Life and Life's effluence, cloud at once and shower." In fiction thus conceived matter and form are not elements conjoined in a structure of counterpoised stresses; they are manifest functions of organic process, mirroring the existence of man as circumstanced consciousness, action as the mode of purposeful and feeling choice, and therefore attitude as the supreme action, because ultimately decisive. To gather up this continuously felt interplay into the work of fictional art is to provide, therefore, a narrative continuity and momentum of the utmost authenticity and persuasiveness.

If then Faulkner's fictional methods, beyond their intricate and beguiling plot structures, are seen as modes in the expression of concern, a peculiarly deep empathy becomes the reader's privilege. Events are rehearsed to be discriminated; the arrival at judgments on ethical bases is a primary activity for certain of Faulkner's characters, especially Gavin, Ratliff, and Charles, and as such it becomes central to the dramatic illusion. With purely objective fiction the reader watches the action and supplements it with his appraisals, toward which the presentation has guided him, but without definition of issue, much less any rendition of verdict. Faulkner's detailed accounts of his spectators' evaluation of others' behavior might, by strict comparison, be considered less artistic. But a more comprehensive estimate, acknowledging Faulkner's undeniable effect on readers' imaginations, may concede that evaluation in itself has been made into a basic narrative factor, judgment considered as a climax of a character's experience. To show it forth is to reveal human behavior at its most vital, sometimes in its most intense crises, often in its most characteristic and revealing commitments. When naturalism, attempting to be as scientific as possible, pauses in an allegedly neutral picturing of behavior and goes no further, it lacks fullest interest as art. Behavior becomes dramatic only when considered as conduct. Only in terms of value judgments does issue become urgent; it is not enough that an event be clearly shown, it must be arranged under the aspect of a literal *cui bono*. To bring the evaluative scrutiny of actions openly and fully into the narrative action itself is to carry the imaginative reader into a fuller participation. Observation as behavior, judgment as conduct—in showing the reader these through his spectators, Faulkner also allows the reader a more empathetic entrance into the whole fable. Faulkner's novels create a many-linked unbroken connection, therefore, between work of art and aesthetic response; Flem, Mink, Eula, and Linda all have their more or less discernible motivations and moods; these are further searched into and evaluated by Gavin, Ratliff, and Charles, whose observation is part of their behavior and whose judgment is central to their conduct; the reader is brought closer by finding these other "readers" in the novel; yet they are not spectators only, they are active interventionists, which involves them further not just with the other characters they confront, but with the reader as now fully enlisted witness, judge, and advocate. Such aesthetic interconnections established within the work by the characters' evaluation as an action in itself enhancing the observed overt action are of course nothing new in either fiction or drama; the remarkable thing is Faulkner's full, open use of such a method, and its intense effectiveness for many readers. The appeal will of course be relative to various factors, including the acuteness and persistence of the reader's ethical concern. This is the point, with Faulkner as also with Conrad, at which response is determined and where admiration will or will not be elicited. The reader who shares Faulkner's kind of concern, together with the assumptions from which it operates, will not only accept Faulkner's dramatization of inquiry and appraisal, he will value it as fictional penetration to the heart of the matter. The brilliant attainment of this large end in the trilogy *Snopes* is justification of its means, an intricate and variegated narrative movement, and in particular its use of the commentators, with their wide-ranging speculations intent on the achievement of humane judgments.

4

"it was not a monument: it was a footprint"

A special effect of Montgomery Ward's appearance as perturbed witness is the emphasized contrast with Flem, setting him off as primate of all Snopesdom. As to the Snopes tribe, Ratliff in *The Town* had said they removed themselves "from just a zoological category . . . by means of the simple rule and regulation and sacred oath of never to tell anybody how" (*T*, 107)—this apropos of Byron's getting himself discharged from the army. But Mink, though craftily secretive, is human by more than that, in playing the game according to his bare beliefs, with a kind of punctilio, and this is presented throughout the third-person chapters he figures in. His conscience, under his limitations of experience and perception, is more primitive than Montgomery Ward's, but it works. He will not steal (*M*, 274), nor will he take advantage of another's mistake in making change (*M*, 261) when he badly needs the money to buy gun and ammunition for killing Flem. To Lump the storekeeper (a minor and more elementary Snopes) it is incredible that Mink did not look in the murdered Houston's pockets for money (*H*, 268), but Mink is above that, nor will he take money his wife has prostituted herself for when he is on the run after the murder (*H*, 276). In accepting the arranged discharge from prison he receives the two hundred and fifty dollars sent by Linda on her condition that he get out of Mississippi and stay out, but on his way he slips the money to a trusty for return to the warden (*M*, 384 ff.); he will pursue his intended revenge and to that end will seize his freedom on a pretext, but he will not keep money taken under false pretenses. Finally, though a needy old fugitive after murdering Flem, he will not accept more money from Linda until Stevens agrees with him that in doing so he "aint promised nobody nothing" (*M*, 433). Mink's scruples are simple and his fidelity to them has about it a kind of fierce Anglo-Saxon strictness. Montgomery Ward's more subtle hesitancies have no such authority for him; he is capable of some sentiment but he cannot rise to consistent conduct. Since Mink's behavior is principled (however primitive his concepts) and even his most violent acts are assertions of honor without regard for practical advantage, he retains sturdiness, his will supported by a limited but sufficient sense of *amour propre*. That is something beyond Montgomery Ward, with all his brashness; he seems nauseated at last by his own iniquities. As with that other typical opportunist, the glib I. O. Snopes, a lack of center leaves him inadequate in a crisis, but whereas I. O. grows panicky Montgomery Ward merely succumbs.

Flem does neither. His steadfastness, however, is of its own kind and in no way admirable. Unlike Mink and even more unlike Montgomery Ward, Flem seems the ultimate of the amoral, so much so that he can scarcely be accounted cruel, being merely insensitive, literally ruthless. It is thereby that he becomes a pivotal point in the trilogy's structure and theme. Recurrently appearing throughout, he is also felt as an almost ubiquitous presence, by his impingements upon the affairs and the apprehensions of others. Unique and just this side the incredible in his absoluteness, he is also paradoxically the very archetype of his tribe and kind, the monolithic image beside whom all other Snopeses are lesser creatures on the scale of Snopesism. Their elements assembled in him are as if chemically modified in another compound, transmuted into the completely inhuman, utterly stable beyond influence or appeal. Flem thus is an ultimate and invariable point of reference, the one whom all the others watch, the figure who haunts all other minds yet whose mind is never seen into, the object to which the variously subjective modes of the trilogy are related. This disposition is indeed one of the central factors in a splendid narrative strategy. It is also suggestive of a dark minor theme, that beyond immorality is a worse end toward which it drifts, amorality. Flem's relative poise in *The Mansion* is to be seen then as arrival unchallenged at this unamenable end. In *The Town* Flem was still on the make, shrugging off the scandal of the stolen brass, deporting other less "respectable" Snopeses from Jefferson, using his wife's affair with De Spain to consolidate his position in the bank, keeping Linda at home to prevent Eula's leaving him and his consequent loss of a hold on her father's bank stock. In *The Mansion* Flem has weathered all that; he has De Spain's house and his bank presidency; Eula, driven to suicide by anxiety over the effect of scandal on Linda and by that boredom which Ratliff named and Gavin wept over, is buried beneath the ironic epitaph to a virtuous wife (*T*, 355)—the irony not consciously Flem's, however, but more of his brazening it out, gaining appearances of respectability in terms which would mean shame to most men, even, perhaps, to Montgomery Ward.

Thus with meretricious status attained and with Mink's vengeance hedged against by treachery, the always laconic Flem, never heard except in an objective setting down of his crafty, clipped speech, is heard even less frequently in *The Mansion.* His only philosophy an expedient acquisitiveness, he can do with almost as little talk as an intent poker player —"the old fish-blooded son of a bitch," as Charles sees him, "who had a vocabulary of two words, one being No and the other Foreclose" (*M,* 215–16). With no pride based on any sense of self—which Mink does have, in simple but definite terms—Flem is incapable of taking evil for his good and is never prompted to a nihilistic role, as of a Jason Compson crying out against man's law and God too (*SF,* 382). Flem recognizes an order, but not as did that other poor white, Sutpen of *Absalom, Absalom!* with his fanatic "design" by which he stubbornly hoped to come to terms with his society and with himself in and of it; Flem, having no intimation of ideal values, merely persists, with never any fretting like Sutpen's over what he cannot understand. So low an aim as Flem's allows complete success, but what he arrives at is the posture of feet propped on the ledge he has had nailed to the Adam mantel, himself inert, lacking even the dark pleasure of a sense of profanation.

When Mink enters Flem merely lowers his feet and swerves in his chair while the pistol misses fire the first time; the action has entered the arena of conduct under principled conviction, where Flem, knowing nothing to do, has nothing to say. One can scarcely agree with Professor Geoffrey Moore that at the end "Flem sits still like some ancient hero resigned to his fate,"[1] nor with Professor Elizabeth Kerr that "Flem, by failing to act and by dying with dignity, gains a

---

[1] *Kenyon Review,* Vol. XXII, No. 3 (Summer, 1960), 520.

moral advantage over the chief critics of his actions."[2] It is
scarcely out of a sense of dignity or with any appearance of
it that Flem fails to resist Mink under those circumstances;
his inertness most emphatically marks an absence in him not
only of heroism in the ancient mold but of primary human
traits and responses. What makes Flem so peculiarly perni-
cious is this seemingly congenital insensitivity, the basis of
his literal inhumanity. Accordingly throughout the trilogy,
and especially in *The Mansion,* Faulkner treats him flatly, in
a two-dimensional narration, as if there were not only no
conscience to be heard but scarcely a consciousness except
as oriented with animal-like instinct toward the only advantage he credits. Here among these many Faulkner characters
so tortured by complexity in themselves and in society is this
paragon of the simple life, the extreme instance of that class
of the unresponsive, the humanly undeveloped to whom the
appeals of civility, ameliorative concession, and graciousness
are inaudible, and whose obstructions of justice and nicety
are as meaningless and as devastating as a stone in a fine-
geared machine. This phenomenon, conspicuous enough to
be imperatively part of the realist's subject, is as tellingly set
forth in the Snopes saga as anywhere in modern fiction. Nor
is anything in Faulkner's portrait of Flem as its arch-exam-
ple more to the point than the consistently objective narrative treatment, with its implication that closer scrutiny could
perhaps dissect a vertebrate nervous system conditioned to
salivate at the smell of money, with what Ratliff called "his
pure and simple nose" for it "like a preacher's for sin and
fried chicken" (*M,* 56), but otherwise content to munch on
air. Indeed, what voice could be found for the night-
thoughts of the creature with his feet against the Adam

[2] *Wisconsin Studies in Contemporary Literature,* Vol. I, No. 2 (Spring-
Summer, 1960), 83.

mantel, as if in reptilian hibernation until time to open the bank again?

But this fellow has a history, not without vicissitude, and in the varied lights of Faulkner's circling presentation he is not only the plainest of villains but often rudely comic and at some few moments almost pitiable, despite his cold-blooded offenses. Appearing in *The Hamlet* as the son of Ab the barn-burner, Flem is seen as "a broad flat face" with eyes "the color of stagnant water" (25), "a thick squat soft man" with "a tight seam of mouth" and "a tiny predatory nose like the beak of a small hawk" (59). The eyes are "opaque" (*T*, 4), they are like "gobs of cup grease" (*T*, 22), and later young Charles remarks that "you couldn't see behind Mr Snopes's eyes because they were not really looking at you" (*T*, 166), and adds that " that was our trouble with Mr Snopes: there wasn't anything to see even when you thought he might be looking at you" (*T*, 167). Pushing his way into a clerk's job at Varner's store on the implied understanding that he would restrain his father's tendency to arson, Flem supplemented storekeeping by trading livestock and by petty usury (*H*, 70) and other more complicated deals, meanwhile bringing in the disreputable relatives he deputized in his assault on the hamlet's economy, until Jody Varner was driven to ask in a shaking voice, "How many more is there? . . . Just what is it going to cost me to protect one goddam barn full of hay?" (*H*, 76). Established at the store, Flem moved into the Varner house as boarder, and when the Varners found Eula pregnant and her suitors scattered, Flem was at hand for his next move, and they "married her to him," a person who for her "had never been" (*H*, 168)—"the splendid girl with her beautiful masklike face" joined to "the froglike creature" (*H*, 169) so that murmurs of regret move across the community, and Ratliff's more detached reflections on Eula as fatal woman merge into the surrealistic mystery-play of Flem in hell, besting even the Prince of Darkness in a fantastic dicker that begins with the failure to find more of Flem's mortgaged soul than a smear in a matchbox and ends when the Prince, told that what the imperturbable Flem wants is hell, screams to him to take Paradise (*H*, 175).

Too few months after the wedding Flem sends Eula and a baby back from Texas, but he does not return until later, and when he comes he brings the notorious spotted horses. Auctioning these, by proxy, and perpetrating his hoax of buried silver that let him sell the Old Frenchman's place which was part of the dowry deal in marrying Eula, he is ready for town and its larger opportunities. He begins there with the cheap restaurant he had traded Ratliff and Grover Cleveland Wimbush out of (*T*, 14), but he has more valuable assets, not unnegotiable. Mayor Manfred de Spain, having set eyes on Eula, put Flem into the specially created office of power-plant superintendent (*T*, 14), in which Flem over-reached himself, making away with brass scrap that included the safety valves on the boilers. In the farcical melee of controverted morality and legality which ensued, everyone, including Gavin Stevens, took some scars except the two Negro firemen Flem meant to use as pawns. His almost successful attempt to turn them against each other led them to the only solution—the way to beat Snopesism, having searched out its machinations, is to join up against it, and it is of some significance that this solidarity is achieved by Negroes of lowly economic as well as social status.

Charles Mallison says of the town's water tank, where the Negroes had dumped Flem's stolen brass, that "it was not a monument: it was a footprint. A monument only says *At least I got this far* while a footprint says *This is where I was when I moved again*" (*T*, 29), and Charles has a point, for

although Flem has been forced to resign the superintendency, he turns up again at the Cotillion Club Christmas Ball,
and Charles reflects how

Jefferson probably thought at first that that rented dress suit was
just the second footprint made on it, until they had time to realise
that it wasn't any more just a footprint than that water tank was a
monument: it was a red flag. No: it was that sign at the railroad
crossing that says Look Out for the Locomotive (*T*, 73).

Flem was not so viewed that night, however. After that
glimpse he is not seen, not even mentioned except negatively
(*T*, 75) as the one who should have protested when De Spain
danced shamelessly with Eula, whereas Gavin intervened,
and tried to fight De Spain afterward, in youthful quixotic
regard for her status, having earlier induced his sister to pro-
cure the Snopeses an invitation to the ball. Flem is almost as
inconspicuous though certainly more active in leaving his
next footprint. In the furore over Byron Snopes's absconding with bank funds Flem emerges as vice-president
while De Spain makes good the losses, the hidden determinant in all these transfers of assets being the wife
and mistress, Eula.

While in *The Hamlet* Snopesism becomes endemic as
Flem brings in one after another of the tribe and finds places
for them and his own uses of them, in *The Town* he becomes
more concerned with ridding Jefferson and himself of them,
in the bid for what Ratliff playfully characterizes as "civic
virtue" (*T*, 175). Flem is busy now exploiting his wife, her
father, her lover, and her daughter, and by playing one interest against another he finally takes over the bank presidency and the De Spain mansion—though the process has
brought Eula to suicide, and Linda has been held as a sort
of hostage until she has seen the marble monument erected
over her mother's grave. What Flem has been up to in all

this, as well as its effects on Eula and Linda, has been and remains Gavin's and Ratliff's chief problem. Ratliff compares it to watching bushes shaken by a varmint and waiting to see where it will come out and what it will do next (*T*, 143). He hits quickly upon the main facts because he sees as merely expedient and acquisitive Flem's manipulations of the interlocked factors: Will Varner's block of bank stock and corresponding power, Eula's claim on the Varner estate, Manfred de Spain's assistance in return for the favor of remaining Eula's unchallenged lover, and the daughter Linda, not Flem's but his pawn too, as the only tie to keep Eula from leaving with De Spain—all these elements employed by Flem for gain and for that pseudo-respectability which will maintain him in the gainful situation. Gavin, with the generous apprehensions of an honorable and imaginative man, extending his speculations further until Ratliff must protest he is missing it (*T*, 153), supposes Flem wants revenge on De Spain (*T*, 318), instead of what material advantage he can take. It is a temptation which may strike the reader, too, to assume that a submerged honor and humanity exist in this creature, and Faulkner has dealt with it through Gavin and Eula. In *The Town*, when Eula discusses with Gavin the hold Flem has tried to establish over Linda and refers to the impotence which symbolizes his isolation from all affectional life, she remarks that "You've got to be careful or you'll have to pity him" (*T*, 331). In *The Mansion*, after the murder, Gavin tells Ratliff of Flem's impotence and pronounces the only elegy for him and others like him who lack the power to love and give, by saying, "The poor sons of bitches that have to cause all the grief and anguish they have to cause" (*M*, 430). This side of pity, with a sort of love, Linda as a girl had indeed fallen partly under Flem's sway, in her desire for a father and her innocence about particular facts and evil in general. Flem attempted some semi-paternal gestures, but when these and other conciliatory moves of his are reëxamined by Gavin, Charles, or Ratliff, they are seen as part of his cold drive toward power and possession, to be supported by a contrived social status sufficient for a banker.

This is evident enough from the trilogy, but Faulkner himself, at the University of Virginia, saw fit to substantiate it in answer to questions; he said he "never did feel sorry for him [Flem] any more than one feels sorry for anyone who is ridden with an ambition or demon as base as simple vanity and rapacity and greed" (*FU,* 120). Flem assumed respectability, said Faulkner, "when he found out that he would need respectability, that just greed, rapacity, wasn't enough" (*FU,* 109) to let him gain what he wanted. As for any hidden pathos in this character, his author apparently does not feel it, for Faulkner also said that Flem "probably understood all of his life that he ever needed to understand" (*FU,* 109). In Flem there is nothing of the more human need to understand, to communicate, to reconcile. His pursuit of "respectability" therefore is as calculating as his greed, of which it is instrument, and if it serves that, this is all he needs to understand about it.

It is of a lower order, too, than the respectability sought by that other upstart, Thomas Sutpen in *Absalom, Absalom!* Building "the largest edifice in the county, not excepting the courthouse itself" (39), Sutpen is intent, according to General Compson, upon "a great deal more than the mere acquisition of a chatelaine for his house" (37). In that what moves him seems a "fierce and overweening vanity or desire for magnificence or for vindication" (38), he shows a kind of honor, too, which makes him want to pay his way at every step, as when in his early days on his unfinished plantation he drank his guests' liquor "with a sort of sparing calculation as though keeping mentally, General Compson said, a sort of balance of spiritual solvency between the amount of whiskey he accepted and the amount of running meat which he supplied to the guns" (40). Flem, on the other hand, is not seen to have any concept of himself which would call for vindication, "spiritual solvency" is a notion he seems never to have entertained, and anything which may look like a humane gesture is seen, looked into, as nothing more than shrewd public relations, as in *The Hamlet*, when he refuses Mrs. Armstid the money the Texan had wanted returned to her after Henry's accident with the wild horse, and then gives her the "small striped paper bag" of cheap candy from the store for her needy children, as "A little sweetening for the chaps" (*H*, 362).

The store clerk Lump Snopes, having received the nickel Flem punctiliously hands over for the candy, slaps his thigh in laughter and says, "By God, you cant beat him" (*H*, 363). In a sense it is true, because no one can quite meet Flem on the level at which he operates, much less communicate with him in any terms. He is a man so isolate in his onward drive and at the same time so hedged about by craft that he literally cannot be dealt with. He is only very rarely caught short, and then he will bargain laconically for whatever advantage he can still take, but with no concession to principle, for he recognizes none. While Flem's very simplicity makes him central, the precise focus of concern, his centrality is not too dominant, because he himself is so limited. It takes Gavin Stevens a while and some effort to see this; he had tried to understand Flem in normal terms, in imagining him the outraged husband capable of vengeance for jealousy, although Ratliff suggested repeatedly that Flem's "civic virtue" is purely materialistic. The finally clarified distinction is emphasized when Gavin Stevens, at the close of the episode in which Flem has forced Montgomery Ward to trick Mink, wryly suggests, "What you are interested in is justice," and Flem answers, "I'm interested in Jefferson. We got to live here" (*T*, 176). The remark is perfectly "respectable" and as perfect a shield for self-interest devoid of principle.

Thus Flem becomes a point of reference by contrast. His inhumanly neutral amorality emphasizes the ethical acuteness of his opponents. His imperviousness to any transcendent concept separates him even from other malefactors. Sutpen's "design," while grandiose and fiercely pursued, at least involved the cultural values of the family, partially appreciated, and this elemental idealism in Sutpen allows Faulkner to name him as one of his "tragic" characters (*FU*, 119). Jason Compson, furiously taking evil for his good, is still dealing in values, although inversely, and acquires thereby that tinge of the tragic found in proudly obsessed sinners. Flem has no such large dimensions as Sutpen's, nor Jason's somber coloration. Indeed, as he is no hero in the classic sense or any other, so he is hardly a conventional villain either; he is so all of a piece that he scarcely can be said to have a flaw or faults. Is this an oversimplification, then, or has Faulkner presented a more special kind of antagonist, one whom humane traditions of conduct and taste have never touched and will never affect? And is not this amoral creature a more specifically modern kind of villain, the ethical nihilist? Sutpen feels dimly that General Compson, representing virtues of a traditional society, may be able to tell him why his "design" has failed; thus even though he does not fully understand it and has been seduced by its grosser aspects, he has recognized the existence of a system of values. Jason, in shaking his fist at the heavens, at least has a sense of defying something conceived of as an order, not without authority. Flem lacks the delinquent's jealous sense of inferiority, the beatnik's self-hypnotic self-consciousness, the revolutionist's galvanizing incantation of ideology. There is no indication that, beyond knowing only what he needs to know, he possesses a sense of identity or of personal conduct. Being neither idealist nor sensualist, he cannot be appealed to at either of those extremes of human experience, as Ratliff imagined the Prince of Darkness himself discovering (*H,* 174). Flem is, even more than Popeye, the modern automaton bred by materialism out of original crudeness. As such he is implacable, and therefore beyond a certain point he is not to be tolerated. His particular nature as villain affects not only the responses of Faulkner's protagonists but their deepest moods; it is Flem's opaque incommunicativeness which prompts both their very modern desperation and their recurrent resolution. In all, it sets the fable on a broad conceptual base and at the same time gives it a peculiarly contemporary flavor, in a period when humane men's several chief enemies are intransigent and impervious.

Appropriately Faulkner treats Flem in shadings of monochrome. This creature has, for instance, a recurrent gesture— he spits, from whatever he is chewing on, tobacco or air and his unremitting intention. His spitting is not just a necessary, almost involuntary vulgarity; it is a refusal of any demand upon him, and its arc traces a separation. Evading Mrs. Armstid's request for the five dollars the Texan had refunded on the purchase of the horse that injured Henry, Flem "raised his head and turned it slightly again and spat neatly past the woman" (*H,* 360). Later, when the bailiff tried to serve a summons on him, Flem denied responsibility, "first turning his head slightly aside to spit" (*H,* 367). So Ratliff had fancied Flem in hell, before Satan's throne, "chewing, toting the straw suitcase," and when the Prince said, "Well?"

Flem "turned his head and spit, the spit frying off the floor quick in a little blue ball of smoke" before he answered, "I come about that soul"—his that is nothing but a dried-up smear, that he never denied was hell's own—and when the Prince tried to bribe him, with every appeal to average sensuality, he just "turned his head and spit another scorch of tobacco onto the floor" (*H*, 174). It is all Frenchman's Bend that he rejects, having used it up, when at the end of *The Hamlet* he "spat over the wagon wheel" (*H*, 421) and then drove on. And whether the gesture refuses to recognize any claim upon him either under the law or in common humanity, whether it is Mrs. Armstid or the bailiff, Flem turns his head just "slightly," so that it is a near thing, at the nice point where defiance is joined to craft.

For all his rise to respectability, Flem retains the gesture. After Eula's suicide Flem holds Linda in Jefferson until they can drive to the cemetery (with Linda's new bags packed and in the car) to see the completed monument to "A Virtuous Wife," Linda not looking at it, sitting with white-gloved hands clenched, and then Flem, chewing tobacco, "leant a little and spit out the window" and said, "Now you can go" (*T*, 355). Linda, long detained at home, had served his purpose, to keep Eula from leaving him, and this further postponement of Linda's departure has been Flem's gesture not of love but of power, implementing the pretense of that monument which, as "a part of what he had come to Jefferson for" (*T*, 349), as Ratliff sees it, needs no price mark "because what it was saying was exactly how much it was worth to Flem Snopes" (*T*, 354), to which imputation his spitting puts a declarative point.

That Flem's vulgar act is not altogether a physical reflex but punctuates his insistent purposes is defined by its absence in a last encounter when Stevens, involved along with

Linda in Mink's parole, and seeking to avert more violence, warns Flem that Mink is at large; now Flem does not move "save for a faint chewing motion," and Stevens thinks, "If he would only spit now and then. . . . Or even just go through the motions of spitting now and then" (*M*, 380), and later, "If he would just spit once" (*M*, 381), while Flem, immobilized at last, merely replies repeatedly, "Much obliged" (*M*, 380, 381), not in appreciation but in dismissal. The impasse at which Flem has arrived illustrates him as a flat character but also contributes to his representativeness of all those whose aggressions can brave it out only so long as their victims shrink from retaliating with equal force. And that the fellow who seemed unbeatable has come to the point where he cannot even spit marks the plainest of finalities.

Still Faulkner, while maintaining Flem as a monolithic character, has caught him in certain different slants of light and finds a way of variation in the portrayal from movement to movement of the trilogy. In *The Hamlet* Flem emerges with a plodding acquisitiveness that is to become sinister as its scale increases. His implacability is already plain; Ratliff tells himself that Mrs. Armstid "cant possibly actually believe" Flem would relent, and adds, "Anymore than I do" (*H*, 362). Flem's three flashiest coups in *The Hamlet*—his marriage deal for Eula with the Varners, his importation and sale of the spotted horses with the Texan as front man, and his selling Ratliff, Bookwright, and Armstid (407) the Old Frenchman's place which he has salted with buried silver—are told with more or less humor but in fundamentally melancholy passages, especially as to the victimizing of Eula Varner and Mrs. Armstid, and also as to Flem's playing on and profiting by others' weaknesses. What jesting there is by onlookers about any of these transactions is sardonic, and in this grim atmosphere the clerk Lump Snopes is the only one who is amused by his own suggestion that "you cant beat him" (*H*, 356, 363). In *The Town,* while Flem continues to rise in the world, chiefly by despicable use of his wife as a Varner and as De Spain's mistress, he does experience a setback and some losses, and these are treated in a more freely comic vein, which allows a natural zest in seeing the climber slip and stumble, with at least some slight skinning. The episode of the stolen brass fixtures from the power-plant boilers balances off several forces. There is Flem's greed becoming folly that would deny the fact of dangerous steam pressure and overreaching itself into a ludicrous impasse which would have shamed any man with a shred of honor. There is the contribution of the two Negro firemen to Flem's defeat when he has attempted to turn one against the other through jealousy, and this is set forth as cabin bedroom farce but also as something more, the power of these intuitive, finally coöperative Negroes to cope with a trashy white man so callous that he cannot sense when he is overplaying his hand. The episode of I. O. Snopes's mule in the yard, with the consequent burning down of the Widow Hait's house and Flem's indemnifying her for her loss, is made into broad folk humor. This is appropriate in its way and place, and for a combination of reasons relating to plot and theme as well. Since Hait had been killed while in I. O. Snopes's employ setting up mules for the night freight to hit, and since I. O. had been quarreling with Hait's widow for part of the indemnity, Flem knows if she now sues over loss of her house, I. O.'s bilking of the railroad company, an open scandal anyhow, would become a matter of court record. To defend the "respectability" Flem must acquire, he appeases Mrs. Hait and buys up I. O.'s mules on condition that he get out of Jefferson. I. O.'s comic defeat is given fillip by the cost to Flem, when for once he paid though for once he apparently had nothing to do with the malfeasance; still Flem's shrewdness is suggested, for in canceling the mortgage so that Mrs. Hait can rebuild with "whatever the insurance company pays" (*T*, 251–52), as he puts it, Flem may be speculating that it would not cover the mortgage. In a third comic episode, Byron's sending his four half-breed children back to Flem, there is a raucous poetic justice, since it was Byron's absconding which had shaken the bank enough to let Flem pry his way in as vice-president. What the incursion of Byron's brood costs Flem is not only the five hundred dollars damages for the pedigreed dog they caught and cooked over a campfire; there is again the matter of reputation befitting a banker. But before he can send them back to El Paso, tagged as when they came like a shipment of livestock, they have busily demonstrated in a kind of nightmarish farce that with a Snopes of any breed no one knows what next but everyone had better look out. It is the outrageous become the ludicrous, and whether this comedy is seen in Freudian terms or as more nearly the classic kind of relief, it adds to the variegated texture of the trilogy while at the same time rounding out theme with recurrence to Flem at the center.

So Charles Mallison in *The Town*, speaking on hearsay from Cousin Gowan of his uncle's earlier discussions of the Snopeses, says Gavin's "main job in telling it was to keep it from being as funny as it really was," because if he let it be that, "everybody and himself too would be laughing so hard they couldn't hear him" (*T*, 45). Here Gavin is the mirrored image of Faulkner himself, and of his readers as they may be. Here the shrug denies for a moment the weight of the burden, the jibe refuses the tribute of terror to the terrible, and the distinction sometimes colloquialized as *funny-ha-ha* or *funny-peculiar* is ambiguously played upon, in acknowledgment that the intricacies of life elicit complex response. A main point, once more, is the mood of it. This is reality; jesting is one way men confront difficulty and declare their refusal to be wholly overborne by it, and the act is always tinctured with consciousness of psychological and moral complexity which sense Faulkner richly reproduces.

The variation in shadings of Flem's essentially simple figure is continued throughout the trilogy. Beyond the bare unimpeded ruthlessness in *The Hamlet* and the comic setbacks in *The Town,* costly but not basically preventive, Flem arrives in *The Mansion* at a fairly fixed status. With position and possessions that give leverage for further gain he has all he wants, and a primitive conservatism masks his operations. He is still ingenious and ruthless, however, as is shown by his handling of Montgomery Ward. He is more wily, though the banker in the black hat does not now stoop to any such crudity as his outright theft of the brass. Now he is advantaged enough to operate more obscurely, and his money power lets him perfect that employment of agents which he had begun with the importation of his relatives in *The Hamlet* and continued more widely in *The Town.* It is perhaps this long-tentacled insidiousness of Flem's in the use of other human beings—brought to perfection and payoff with Varner, De Spain, Montgomery Ward, and Eula and Linda through each other—which more than anything else reveals his amorality and puts him beyond pity. In *The Mansion* the shadings become darker, the grotesqueness of Flem is more than ever that of the unremitting exploiter, and whether in the banker's chair or in the pillared house with his feet propped against the mantel, he is still a pivotal figure but fixed in perspective. The comic in the struggle with Snopesism is transferred in this third volume to the minor figure of Clarence and his defeat by Ratliff, through means as devious as any Flem ever devised, but more imaginative, blending with acrid dog-scent the very essence of poetic justice. As for Flem, he scarcely needs a relative in political office now, and he remains a Snopes whom not even Uncle Billy Varner can dump. Flem's instigations are from a greater distance, and laconic as ever, he never testifies against himself. In *The Mansion* Faulkner has isolated and immured Flem, as inhumanly remote from comedy as from tragedy, in a tale that abounds in both.

If Flem's absolute insensitivity, emphasized by contrast with Mink's primitive sense of honor and Montgomery Ward's negative grace of uneasy conscience, is one extreme, Gavin Stevens' chivalry is the other. Gavin is abetted but not duplicated by Ratliff and Charles; other Snopeses of different stripe enter the action; and there are the two implicated women, Eula Varner Snopes and Linda, a Snopes by name only, figuring strangely between two worlds. The struggle begun in *The Hamlet* with Ratliff as the leading opponent of Snopesism, and continued through *The Town* with Gavin Stevens as the only partially successful champion of Eula and Linda, broadens in *The Mansion* to pit a Snopes in mortal enmity against Snopesism, and to involve Gavin Stevens even more personally than in *The Town*. As before, the shadings of character are infinite. Apart from Flem there are no complete villains, and among the well-intentioned there are no conventionally infallible lone rangers or Robin Hoods. In *The Mansion* even more than in the two preceding volumes, Faulkner's discriminations impel multifarious development, crowding his stage with diverse character and incident, but always interrelated, in a counterpointing of values or variation on motifs. The discomfiting of Clarence Snopes as political candidate is robust folk humor, with Ratliff the deftly devising interventionist. Orestes Snopes appears as merely another family agent of Flem's acquisitiveness, which

runs through former Compson acres to encounter old Meadowfill's cantankerous resistance and requires the intuitive
Gavin's quick intervention to prevent violence impinging
upon Meadowfill's daughter and her husband. These episodes, while thematically related to the trilogy, are self-con-
tained actions. Linda, on the other hand, moves throughout
this third volume as a main figure, and one with an appearance of doom, to whom Charles repeatedly applies the sad
word "Lost" (*M*, 219, 222), and whose all but hopeless status
(with the mansion for home and Flem for family) involves
Gavin not only as civilized champion of principle but as
compassionate man caught up in a sustained personal relationship as foil to Flem's inhumanity.

With the elements thus so diversely mixed in *The Mansion* as capstone, and with entanglements running back into
the trilogy's preceding events and beyond, some discussion
may turn on whether *Snopes*, Faulkner's most extended
work, is a conglomerate miscellany or has been rounded into
a genuine composition, intricate yet organized. That it is the
latter should appear if the theme of existence in a world
permeated by Snopesism is fully credited, and if the variety
of men's responses to aspects of Snopesism is broadly looked
at. In this light even the most tangential developments may
be seen to substantiate that massive reality a "big" novel
must encompass: the nature of individual being and rela-
tionships in a crowded and sometimes disordered milieu, in
which values are forever in jeopardy, while conduct must
find its way through confusions and face up to inherent
antitheses, and although the acceptance of half a loaf must
stipulate that it be not a stone, the price of immunity from
despair is the foregoing of certain illusions, including that of
anyone's infallibility, no matter how well-intentioned.

In the trilogy as a complex—multiform in substance and

an intricate artistic composition—the plainly two-dimensional, opaque squat figure of Flem shows how such a grotesque can be made a primary element in a thematically conceived work of realism. Flem is forever shifty, but as a point of reference he does not shift. He remains a very present evil, an absolute against which all combative efforts remain relative. Hence the pertinence of the inclusive title *Snopes*. Nor with his death is Snopesism dead; it is perennially a condition, which the local instances not only picture but typify. As an inescapable factor of the actual, this is that which good will must repeatedly confront or lose its will, must live with without accepting, must face or else lose sight of reality, must always contain and restrain as may be, although doing so, under the aspect of mutability, without expectation of lasting success. As surely as the sun rises and sets evil-doing recurs, a fact of nature; against this the humane is but tentative, and its repeated assertion out of magnanimity and courage, if this too be part of reality, is likewise enigmatic and a matter for faith. Yet with all its aggression given utmost scope by ruthlessness, evil as an absolute has a static quality, whereas benevolence and beneficence, while relative, are also dynamic. Flem, for all his being on the make, remains the same, as in the vignettes of the continuous chewing and the inert state with feet against the mantelpiece. Conversely Faulkner's men of good will and well-doing, for all their bafflement, are those whose motion, ethically purposeful, gives the fiction breath and pulse and the pace of life, and whose principled intention most profoundly validates the composition as realism, a total realism, actual complexity, full of the knowledge of good and evil endlessly interworking, in that magnitude to be comprehended only through the tragic sense of life.

5

"We have had everything"

In *The Mansion* the greatest complexity, occasioning the most prolonged pondering by Ratliff and Charles, centers in Linda and Gavin. Object of his intense concern, she is the strangest of heroines, forlorn by heredity and diverse event, yet resolute and thereby the more appealing. In *The Town* Gavin had sought to save the girl not only from the notoriety of a name but from Snopes himself, who had seemed as ready to exploit the nominal daughter as the calculatingly acquired wife. Ironically Gavin's manipulations which got Linda out of Flem's control and off to New York then let her be married and carried to Spain at war, from which, bereaved and totally deafened, she returns more than ever Gavin's unofficial ward. She remains so none the less although during the years of World War II, while Linda works in a shipyard, Gavin has wed his long-time secret love, the widowed Melisandre.

98

Any assumption like the one made by Anthony West in *The New Yorker*[1] that in "Knight's Gambit" Faulkner had wastefully married off his favorite protagonist to Melisandre Backus Harriss and then was stuck with an incredibility in Gavin's continuing particular relationship with Linda in *The Mansion* seems an impercipiently conventional reading. Gavin's chivalry is not to be conceived of as either monogamous or promiscuous; it exists in other terms. Quite conscious of sexual appeal, Linda's as well as Eula's, Gavin feels still more strongly the need to defend these women from Snopes, and if possible to rescue Linda from him. Gavin's relations with Melisandre, as traced in "Knight's Gambit" and alluded to in *The Town,* make it a different case. In 1919, knowing that "just silence" at war's "red and stinking corridor's end . . . was not peace" (*KG*, 233), Gavin romantically betroths himself to the lovely innocent Melisandre Backus, isolated on her widower father's impoverished plantation. She is to have time, they correspond when Gavin goes back to Heidelberg, but his letter to a former mistress is mistakenly addressed to Melisandre, and soon thereafter she marries Harriss, older, of dubious reputation, but on the make financially. The mischance throws light not only on that marriage as an expedient and perhaps fatalistic second choice, but on Gavin's prolonged bachelorhood as mark of a hidden disappointment; and when, after the to-do in "Knight's Gambit" with her grown children and Captain Gualdres, Gavin is able to claim Melisandre, he does so directly. Her wealth is no obstacle; he accepts none of it and thinks nothing of it. What does matter is that she is not only free but maturely his equal, whom he can meet in love without reticence or the kind of anxious fostering he had accorded the inexperienced girl. And Gavin senses such distinctions quite clearly;

[1] December 5, 1959, p. 234.

it is a part of his gentility, a behavior based on a code earnestly held. His principled affectionate relation with Linda is made clearer by the plain fact that there is no obstacle to it or conflict with it in his marriage to Melisandre. Indeed thereafter he and Linda are if anything more closely bound, but both too experienced to be capable of simplicity, so that they move under stresses of circumstance in a sort of pavane stylizing feelings beyond any point of repose, too acute to be dismissed, too inherent in their lives' textures to be escaped, and filled with a paradoxical pathos in which having "nothing" they have "everything" (*M*, 425).

In "Knight's Gambit" young Charles Mallison, introduced by his Uncle Gavin to the widowed Melisandre Backus Harriss (then supposedly being courted by Captain Gualdres) had made a thoughtful distinction which would seem to be Faulkner's own, and which clearly accounts for the ordering of Gavin's affectional life thereafter:

She looked exactly as he had known she would, and then and even before they stopped, he could smell it too: the scent of old sachet, lavender and thyme and such, which, you would have thought, the first touch of the world's glitter would have obliterated, until in the next second you realised that it—the scent, the odor, the breath, the whisper—was the strong and the enduring, and it was the inconstant changing glitter which flashed and passed (163).

It is here, to something enduring thus symbolized, that Gavin's private life as lover and husband is to be attached, the center from which his chivalrous assistance to Linda and others can be extended, with presumably no violation of his deepest personal loyalty to that center, in a fixed passion of which nothing more needs to be told.

Much has already been told, moreover, in the Faulkner chronicle. What Charles in "Knight's Gambit" sees on meet-

ing Melisandre is complementary to what he had partially
perceived earlier, when at Christmas his mother would re-
ceive from the married woman living with her two Harriss
children in Europe

the old-timey cards out of the old time, giving off the faint
whisper of old sentiment and old thought impervious to the foreign names and languages, as if she had carried them across the
ocean with her from a bureau drawer in the old house which
these five and ten years had no longer existed (*KG*, 159).

Then the letters too would come,

still talking not only of the old homely things but in the old un-
changed provincial terms, as if in ten years of the world's glitter
she still hadn't seen anything she had not brought with her
(*KG*, 159).

Thereupon young Charles would watch his Uncle Gavin sitting

holding one of the letters his mother had received, incorrigible
and bachelor, faced for the only time in his life with something
on which he apparently had nothing to say (*KG*, 160),

a silence which Charles has noted in him before, during
Harriss's rebuilding of the Backus place, "the year . . . his
uncle seemed to have stopped talking very much about anything" (*KG*, 155), and which Charles notes again when they
meet the widowed Melisandre on the street and Gavin, assuming she is now committed to Captain Gualdres, is so
awkward that Charles thinks "probably talking was like golf
or wing-shooting: you couldn't afford to miss a day" (*KG*,
164).

While the youth Charles had had those glimpses, and later
in "Knight's Gambit" (232–45) is the one recipient of his
uncle's final confidences about the whole story, including the
wrongly sent letter, Gavin's early love for Melisandre, their

pledging and the subsequent mishap, and his long silent devotion thereafter are matters so deeply personal that apparently he does not confide any of it even to his sister, of whom he asks careful questions to determine that it has remained secret (*KG*, 148). In the trilogy Faulkner has not chosen to refer to it, perhaps because that would have necessitated so detailed a recounting to convey its essence truthfully as to be digressive in effect. If so, it is one more example of careful selectivity in Faulkner's full narrative, where recapitulation, however free, varied, and extended, is always thematic. Criticism of Faulkner for repetitiousness should first take due note of how very much and also what he refrains from recapitulating. It might fancifully be supposed that Faulkner, with Charles, respects Gavin's secrets, but it is plain the novelist has relied on a right perception of Gavin's genuinely chivalrous attitude to Linda, and toward Eula as well, something beyond but not inconsistent with a man's natural response to Eula's stirring beauty and female vitality, that which gives young Charles "a kind of shock of gratitude just for being alive and being male at the same instant with her in space" (*T*, 6), and which Ratliff, for all his coolness, sometimes describes, as in his reference to the medallion fastened to the front of the monument, carved in Italy from a photograph Linda and Gavin had picked out, the face

that never looked like Eula a-tall you thought at first, never looked like nobody nowhere you thought at first, until you were wrong because it never looked like all women because what it looked like was one woman that ever man that was lucky enough to have been a man would say, "Yes, that's her. I knowed her five years ago or ten years ago or fifty years ago and you would a thought that by now I would a earned the right not to have to remember her any more" (*T*, 354–55).

While Faulkner (together with Ratliff and Charles as commentators) does not minimize such a sexual element in Gavin's situation with Eula and with Linda, even up to the point of Linda's final departure (*M*, 423–26), the trilogy has adequately implied another and predominant motivation, Gavin's involvement, as protagonist of the ethical, versus Snopesism, a commitment his moral nature makes the primary imperative, so that indeed, as Ratliff puts it, he was like "a feller out in a big open field and a storm of rain: there aint no being give nor accepting to it: he's already got it" (*T*, 349). And when Charles remarks of Gavin and the widowed Linda that "He can't marry her now" since "He's already got a wife," Melisandre, and Ratliff replies that it's "going to be worse than that" (*M*, 256), what he means is certainly not adultery, but a further quixotic defense of a sadly beset woman against Snopesism, under conditions more complicated and psychologically more severe than ever. While all of Ratliff's remarks about Gavin and women must be salted with the fact that he apparently knew little or nothing of Gavin's early and long attachment to Melisandre, it is always apparent too that Ratliff understands Gavin's chivalric concern, which he jests at for its extremes, respects in its intentions, and abets in practice.

However increasingly difficult Gavin's relations with the returned "lost" Linda, because of her forlorn state and the stimulation of their intimacy by her dependence, he can proceed without inhibition because his marriage is well-founded, a sound reality taken for granted by its partners. That Faulkner allows this centrality to remain beyond description does not make it incredible, nor is the concept too subtle or the situation too mysterious for any who grant the possibility that, after mischance and long delay, such an ideality could be approximated by the right-spirited. While dependent on the reader's intuitive response to this, Faulkner's emphasis seems right artistically, since the theme of the trilogy is Snopesism and its confrontation by Stevens as leading protagonist in *The Town* and *The Mansion*. At this nice critical point concerning fictional composition Faulkner's practice is masterful. And not only is the selective emphasis correct, Gavin's status as happily married man sets into clearest light his championship of another woman. His struggles to protect the unhappily vulnerable from the unprincipled go on in a broad social context, too, and the evil being insistent, no stable peace can be achieved, nor can concern ever subside. Gavin's difficulties are, so to speak, public and recurrent, not private and soluble; his plentiful problems do not include his marriage, the one point where he seems at rest, which is where the trilogy leaves him.

Ratliff's curious review of Gavin's involvement with Linda traces it back to a romantic young man's fascination by her mother, so that this lovechild of Eula and McCarron seems also to Gavin the mystical offspring of his earlier and enduring sentiment. There is a more special imperative, however, which Gavin phrases thus: "To save Jefferson from a Snopes is a duty; to save a Snopes from a Snopes is a privilege" (*T*, 184). His extravagant attentions to young Linda are thus quite other than marks of an inhibited middle-aged lust. The town's cultivated lawyer meeting the naïve and domestically beset high school girl at the soda fountain for conversation over loaned books is a gallant man. It is revealing that Faulkner, in comments at the University of Virginia about his characters' struggles against Snopesism, spontaneously used images connected with chivalry. Saying that "there's always someone that will never stop trying to cope with Snopes," he added that "When the battle comes it always produces a Roland" (*FU*, 34). At another time he called the tendency to resist Snopesism "the old cavalier spirit" and defined its proponents as "people who believe in simple honor for the sake of honor, and honesty for the sake of honesty" (*FU*, 80). Faulkner's Roland is Gavin Stevens, who stands first and unique among several protagonists by virtue of his chivalry. He is Faulkner's man, "always someone that will never stop trying," and Faulkner let him voice precisely that view in *Intruder in the Dust,* as a confirmation of young Charles Mallison's self-won initiation into a virile championship of the defenseless:

Some things you must never stop refusing to bear. Injustice and outrage and dishonor and shame. No matter how young you are or how old you have got. Not for kudos and not for cash: your picture in the paper nor money in the bank either (*ID*, 206).

What had been upheld in that situation was every man's right to justice, without regard for race, color, or any other circumstance; the situation was local, however, and with a particular social reference. Gavin's protection of Linda has a more nearly universal and perennial mode. No mere quaint Southern gentleman of the old school, he is one in whom a traditional regard for womanhood is still vitally part of a humanistic outlook, the personal complement of his philosophically conservative democratic politics, which asks for equity, rational reciprocity, and the necessary sacrifice of self-interest for the sake of ordered values. And as with his politics, his appreciation of woman's place and prerogatives is fraught with anxiousness under the inroads of modern vulgarities as well as ancient recurrent brutalities. (Here again in the trilogy a particular contemporary theme is sounded: the civilized honorable man's frustration and fear in sensing the opponent as not just single but massive, Snopesism as trend, and from below, as tide rising to flood the formal garden and cover its statuary.)

Unconventional as are all Gavin's relations with Linda, from her girlhood on through many a distressing vicissitude, their eccentricity shows chiefly as an opposite to the town's more typical blend of censoriousness and indifference. Gavin's concern centers disinterestedly on emancipating Linda from Flem's control and getting her out of Jefferson, where the shameful terms of her mother's marriage are common knowledge. With his usual inclusiveness Faulkner allows the superficial view as well, which finds a gawky aspect and at the same time something suspect in Gavin's endeavor, and which Charles Mallison's father elaborates in his customarily earthy style. When Charles's mother (Gavin's sister) tries to explain Gavin's interest in Linda, her husband describes the two of them in the ice cream parlor and adds:

Maybe he's concentrating on just forming her form first you might say, without bothering too much yet about her mind. And who knows? Maybe some day she'll even look at him like she was looking at that banana split or whatever it was (*T*, 180).

Gavin himself admits some questionable appearance in his fostering of Linda when he imagines how he, "the middle-aged (whiteheaded too even) small-town lawyer" (*T*, 285), must have looked to Flem: a "menace and threat . . . with his constant seduction of out-of-state school brochures" (*T*, 287). Yet these shadings do not negate the central fact, the honorableness of Gavin's purposes, evoked by Linda's really acute need. His open assignations with a high school girl, awkward as spectacles, are really awkward for both participants, but this is the best that Gavin can do, and it might have helped, for in time he did get Linda freed and on her way. Perhaps she might have been saved thereby, had not war in Spain bereaved and injured her and driven her back to Jefferson and to Flem's mansion, genuinely a returning

veteran in Charles's eyes, and in Gavin's one needing reha-
bilitation.

By that time Linda needed protection too against a community hostile to her for her alliance with a New York Jew
and for their communistic affiliation, which they had classically declared, with such fatality, by joining in the Spanish
Civil War. Moreover, this guilt of hers by direct and ardent
association is then compounded, in local eyes, when she
seeks to develop improved education for Negroes. In that
time and place the Negro school principal—"the intelligent
dedicated man with his composed and tragic face" as Gavin
sees him (*M*, 224)—must send her word that her benevolence
lacks discretion and practicality, while some others convey a
message anonymously but more bluntly, in "the words *Nig-
ger Lover* scrawled huge in chalk on the sidewalk in front
of the mansion" (*M*, 226). Then too Gavin must defend
Linda from a more imposing force, personified by the F.B.I.
agent who

just sat there watching . . . through his glasses, gray, negative as
a chameleon, terrifying as the footprint on Crusoe's beach, too
negative and neuter in that one frail articulation to bear the terrible mantle he represented (*M*, 234–35).

When this agent proposes that Linda secure immunity from
further investigation by giving names of Communists she
and Kohl might have known in New York, Gavin bids him
good day and turns his mind to a more immediate problem,
whether it was Flem himself who had "ransacked" evidence
of Linda's Communist connections out of her "room drawers
desk," to hold that threat over her "to defend his very existence before she destroyed it—the position he had sacrificed
everything for" (*M*, 240). The Battle of Britain saved Linda,
Gavin says (*M*, 244), by prompting her to seek war work, in

a shipyard, for which Gavin advises not California but the Gulf Coast of Mississippi, writing that he could "come there quick" if she were questioned by any "individual of limitless power called Security whose job position is the 1 thing on earth between him & being drafted" (*M*, 245).

Gavin Stevens' sustained protection of the injured, widowed Linda in this first phase after her return to Jefferson reasserts his devotion and elicits a similar reiteration from her. Under conditions vastly altered and all the worse for her, they play out their troubled parts with a complete consistency, faithful to their past in their present fidelity to each other. Naturally in so intimate and mindful a relation some consciousness of the sexual figures, but it does not dominate, and neither Linda's inconsolable grief for her lost husband nor, later, Gavin's deeply based loyalty to his wife precludes a sustained affection which gives reality and integrity to a relationship that on the surface has an artificial look. The key to it is the absolute sincerity of their mutual regard and concern, which Gavin's chivalry and Linda's forthright warmth both declare. And so their history in part repeats itself, but not monotonously, rather with those reaffirmations which are marks of character and evidence of principle.

Had Gavin's earlier interest in the high school girl been sexual, he could have seized upon Eula's suggestion—made first during his struggle to get Linda away to college (*T*, 226), and repeated so bluntly and with such maternal anxiety in the last harried hours of Eula's life (*T*, 330 ff.)—that he give Linda the permanent protection of marriage. But Gavin not only admits himself too old for her, he knows his feelings have been as different from those of a lover as from a father's, nor would he assume it to be merely a question of how he felt about such a marriage. Indeed, before Eula made the expedient suggestion, Linda and Gavin had gone all over the matter, in essence, even though she was only a girl and an innocent one at that. When young Matt, the auto mechanic and Golden Gloves champion, jealously bloodied Gavin's nose, sixteen-year-old Linda slapped Matt and cursed him for a fool and a clumsy ignorant ox and wept over "Mr. Gavin," clinging to him, and when they were alone and he was moved to say, "Do you want to marry me?" she answered, "Yes! Yes! All right! All right!" but when the scrupulous Gavin asks further whether she wants to get married and she finds she doesn't "have to," she says, still clinging closely to him, "I don't want to marry anybody! Not anybody! You're all I have, all I can trust. I love you! I love you!" (*T*, 192, 193).

Certainly in this psychologically subtle and deeply human scene Faulkner has indicated the special nature of their relationship from the first. Linda's dependence is the greater because she is caught in a situation she cannot wholly understand, and there is consequently a greater demand upon Gavin for disinterestedness. It becomes his primary concern to establish her on firmer ground, from which she can and does proceed. If naturally he feels Linda's feminine appeal, as he had felt her mother's, under his code in this situation passion must be subordinated to what he conceives of as his duty, not only to Linda, but to the principles upon which he bases his defense of her. It is easy to ridicule as sentimentally unreal the notion of the naked sword between refraining lovers, but Faulkner for all his propensity for the comic has not found Gavin's chivalry merely amusing, and leaving this lesser aspect of it to Charles's father ("What's the matter, boy? Where's your spear and sword? Where's your white horse?" [*T*, 185]), he has attempted to represent a deep authenticity of conduct, a gallantry that is truly expressive of self and humanly sustaining.

It is part of this reality that Linda, like her mother before her, is slow to understand Gavin's resolute subordination of desire to duty, of the personal to the socio-ethical, and of passion's insistence to a sustained affectional devotion. However extraordinary and whatever its particular direction, this represented reality of idealistic conduct stands opposite to human relationship practiced as mere barter varied by opportunistic encroachment and seizure. Eula Varner Snopes had been allowed little acquaintance with any other view of life than that. Exploitation by parents, husband, and lover has left her almost as fatalistic as Ruby Goodwin in *Sanctuary*, who takes it for granted she must give herself to Horace Benbow in return for his legal services to her accused husband, and to whom Benbow is constrained to say, "But cant you see that perhaps a man might do something just because he knew it was right, necessary to the harmony of things that it be done?" (*S*, 331). Horace Benbow, also lawyer and interventionist, seems Gavin's prototype. In *Sanctuary* (359) he, like Gavin Stevens later in "Knight's Gambit" (164, 165), murmurs a recollected literary phrase— "lest oft is peace"—to ease his strain in a world where victims of evil have lost not only belief in good but any conception of it, another point at which Faulkner touches upon a representative fact that takes on peculiar incisiveness as parallel to contemporary world events. Happenings in Linda's varied life beyond Yoknapatawpha County are the opposite of Eula's completely provincial fate, but whether it be ruthlessness on a Frenchman's Bend scale or the violences of a world war, the devastations are similar for both women. The actions of both, so often tinged with an unconfessed desperation, seem expressive of an irremediable traumatic state, which demands all the more generous disinterestedness from any who would aid them.

Having depended increasingly on Gavin as a sort of foster parent, Linda returns from the war in Spain to offer herself to him out of her experience of life—as long before Eula had offered herself when she thought it was perhaps what Gavin wanted in his conflicts with her lover Manfred de Spain and with Flem Snopes. The scene between Linda and Gavin is typical; each is thinking magnanimously of the other. Gavin, writing on a foolscap pad on the mantel in Linda's room in the mansion (*M*, 237), has advised her to get away again, perhaps back to New York and "some of the people still you and Barton knew," but she is "afraid" of being "helpless," and "just must be" where Gavin is. He writes that she is not to be afraid, he won't marry her, adding, "I Refuse . . . I Dont want to" and she tells him she loves him, this time because "even when I have to tell a lie, you have already invented it for me" (*M*, 238). The lie unspoken mirrors the suppressed truth behind their talk; Gavin writes, "No lie nobody Mentioned Barton Kohl," but Linda says, "Yes," and rightly, for his ghost is in the room, his memory in her mind. "But," says Linda, and proffers herself bluntly (*M*, 238), with the "one bald unlovely" word which, as Gavin writes in reply, shocks because it sums up and dismisses "all that magic passion excitement" (*M*, 239). There follows a close paralleling of the scene (*T*, 192, 193) from her girlhood (after her brash suitor Matt had assaulted Gavin), but this time in adult dialogue, yet with no less understanding on his part or appreciation from her. "Do you mean you want to," Gavin writes, and she merely replies, "Of course you can," and when he insists she answer the question, she is motionless and he sees her looking at him "from out or across what it was that I would recognize in a moment now" before she says, "Yes," whereupon he writes the repeated assurance that she need not be afraid, nor will he insist that she leave

Flem Snopes's mansion and Jefferson, and now he knows "what it was she looked out of or across: the immeasurable loss, the appeaseless grief, the fidelity and the enduring." So he writes that they "can love each other without having to," and now, clinging to him she says again, as she had years before in awareness of his understanding and dependability, "I love you. I love you" (*M*, 239).

Gavin's refusal of women's favors offered under duress of any kind—whether Eula's in her precarious position between nominal husband and lover or the widowed Linda's in her wish to "just be where" Gavin is—conforms with his romantic regard for women (as above all for Melisandre over the many years) and also accords with his idealistic faith in love itself and the possibilities of its realization. To the whole community Eula had seemed a Venus, or at least a Helen, exciting passionate admiration and envy, and then the subject of regret when she was given over to Flem, the Vulcan to this goddess—as the schoolmaster Labove's infatuated imagination had despairingly prefigured her fate while Eula was still a child (*H*, 135)—and when after her suicide Ratliff says, "Maybe she was bored" (*T*, 358), Gavin agrees, and elaborates sadly:

"Yes," he said. "She was bored. She loved, had a capacity to love, for love, to give and accept love. Only she tried twice and failed twice to find somebody not just strong enough to deserve, earn it, match it, but even brave enough to accept it" (*T*, 359).

Gavin has seen too that Linda should have something better:

not her mother's fierce awkward surrender in a roadside thicket at night with a lover still bleeding from a gang fight; but love, something worthy to match not just today's innocent and terrified and terrifying passion, but tomorrow's strength and capacity for serenity and growth and accomplishment and the realisation of hope and at last the contentment of one mutual peace and one mutual conjoined old age (*T*, 288–89).

When for a moment in the midst of multiple circumstance Gavin had even let himself imagine a mystic past identification with young McCarron, making himself not only Linda's father but Eula's lover who had begot the child (*T*, 135), it is the most extreme instance of the romantic in his attachment to these two women, but his more sustained, more rational attitudes toward them are not less intensely felt. Snopesism most acutely affronts and unavoidably challenges Gavin by its victimizing of Eula and its threats to Linda; the magnanimity of Gavin's concern for both Eula and Linda, resting in moral conviction, is the opposite pole to Snopes meanness. On this contrast the trilogy is structurally poised; in these terms Gavin's quixotism, extreme as it is, seems the minimum ameliorative measure and thus the only honorable position this side of compromise.

Therefore even when Gavin's behavior at times seems compulsive, it appears not only a credible but a natural reaction, and theme is broadly enforced whenever he is differentiated from other extremists by the separate natures of their drives. Flem is completely conditioned to a calculating acquisitiveness; Mink's single-minded quest for vindication through revenge is intensified, by its very obstacles, to something like monomania. Sexuality too becomes compulsive for some; the schoolmaster Labove knows he is mad (*H*, 135) in his desire for the adolescent Eula Varner, yet he stays on in the wretched situation, almost as obsessed in his way as is the idiot Ike Snopes in his perversion. While Gavin is neither acquisitive, egotistically assertive, nor lustful, his conduct had seemed to young Gowan as intensely preoccupied, though on broader terms.

It was almost like he was talking to himself, like something wound up that couldn't even run down, let alone stop, like there wasn't anybody or anything that wished he would stop more than he did (*T*, 45).

Gavin defines the involvement when Eula comes to his office, at the time of the stolen brass scandal, which touches Flem as power-plant superintendent, and Manfred de Spain, who appointed him. "We've all bought Snopeses here," he says, "whether we wanted to or not . . . I don't know why . . . what coin and when and where we so recklessly and improvidently spent that we had to have Snopeses too" (*T*, 95). Ratliff, in his own vernacular, paraphrases Gavin's saying much the same thing to him:

"Say a herd of tigers suddenly appears in Yoknapatawpha County; wouldn't it be a heap better to have them shut up in a mule-pen where we could at least watch them, keep up with them, even if you do lose a arm or a leg ever time you get within ten feet of the wire, than to have them roaming and strolling loose all over ever where in the entire country? No, we got them now; they're ourn now; I dont know jest what Jefferson could a committed back there whenever it was, to have won this punishment, gained this right, earned this privilege. But we did. So it's for us to cope, to resist; us to endure, and (if we can) survive" (*T*, 102).

Eula's ambiguous and inescapable captivity in this total situation perhaps has to do with Gavin's refusal of her offer of herself to him; if it is not to call him off and spare either Manfred or Flem or both, is it, he wonders, a kind of pity for himself or only to show him out of her own disenchantment that the sexual is "not even worth being unhappy over" (*T*, 94). Recognizing such continuous fragmentation of values under the reductive impact of Snopesism, Gavin continues to resist it. Nor can he accept Eula's admonition: "You spend too much time expecting. Don't expect. You just are, and you need, and you must, and so you do. That's all. Don't waste time expecting" (*T*, 94). This advice compounded of *carpe diem* and grin-and-bear-it he cannot take, any more than he could have played Manfred's part, the casual lover, and still have been himself, as he admits. For Gavin is possessed purely and intensely by the human attribute of looking before and after, though he has little time to pine for what is not, being so occupied in apprehensively expecting what should not be and seeking to avert it or at least tardily to right some of its wrongs, especially as they impinge upon Linda.

At the end of the trilogy, in the hour after Linda's departure, what remains to accomplish is the final collusion, passing her gift of money to Flem's escaping murderer, Mink, and this is the nadir of Gavin Stevens' experience. Ratliff, musing ironically on how all Flem's "ramshacking and foreclosing and grabbling and snatching" has finally resulted in the return of the mansion, "that-ere big white elephant of a house," to De Spain relatives, "a bedrode old lady and her retired old-maid schoolteacher daughter that would a lived happily ever after in sunny golden California," speculates that "maybe there's even a moral in it somewhere, if you jest knowed where to look," and Stevens says, "There aren't any morals. People just do the best they can," to which Ratliff responds, "The pore sons of bitches," which Stevens repeats with only a shift in pronunciation (*M*, 428–29). He has indeed been pressed to the limit, and hence as they leave Mink in his temporary hide-out with the delivered money, "two old men themselves, approaching their sixties," the ironically humorous Ratliff is given the last word:

"I dont know if she's already got a daughter stashed out somewhere, or if she jest aint got around to one yet. But when she does I jest hope for Old Lang Zyne's sake she don't never bring it back to Jefferson. You done already been through two Eula Varners and I dont think you can stand another one" (*M*, 434).

As usual, Ratliff's simplicities are loaded with implication.

He not only assumes that Gavin would go on "expecting," he seems aware that whatever the outcome, Gavin would not regard expectation according to his values as a waste of time.

Although they disappear from the scene and from the trilogy to the tune of Ratliff's wryness, there are further overtones. Stevens' statement that "There aren't any morals" scarcely denies morality, for he goes on to say people do the "best" they can. Once more Gavin Stevens seems to be speaking with his author's voice. That voice has been heard directly to the same effect in Faulkner's conversations at the University of Virginia. Answering questions there, he said, "Maybe the writer has no concept of morality at all, only an integrity to hold always to what he believes to be the facts and truths of human behavior" (*FU*, 267). Like many of Faulkner's cryptic answers to interviewers, this may be best understood in correlation with other statements. While he said that theme or "message" is one of the literary craftsman's "tools," he added that "you don't write a story just to show your versatility with your tools," but "to tell about people, man in his constant struggle with his own heart, with the hearts of others, or with his environment" (*FU*, 239). He said also that he likes to read the Old Testament because "it's full of people, not ideas" (*FU*, 167). Asked about "virtues," he proposed a "better word . . . the verities of the human heart." These he called "courage, honor, pride, compassion, pity" and said, "One doesn't try to practice them . . . simply because they are good" but "because they are the edifice on which the whole history of man has been founded and by means of which . . . as a race he has endured this long" (*FU*, 133). Faulkner's position is not obscure, nor is it equivocal. The verities he names plainly involve value concepts, but these values are viewed pragmatically, not as detached ab-

tractions; more than merely intellectual propositions theo-
etically arrived at, they exist as realities in some people's
common practice, facts in the human condition.

This distinction as Faulkner made it is a revelation of his
own nature and subtly an apologia for his practice as an
artist. He has always known what some of his contemporar-
es in the thirties fatally neglected, that ideology reduces
and may even emasculate art, by minimizing the charged
polarity between experience and the creative artist's intui-
ions. Repeated remarks of his evince an acute consciousness of his "demon" (*FU*, 204, 205). Respecting the luck of
being so possessed, he seems to distrust any overintellectual-
zing which might reduce spontaneity or carry abstraction
beyond realities. Apparently Faulkner has not sought out
subject matter or observed formally; he has listened often
and long to country people talking, but not "with a note-
book" and not even intentionally, finding simply that "it was
interesting . . . just to remember" (*FU*, 233). Gavin Stevens,
in his brief appearance in *Light in August*, is much the
same: "he can be seen now and then squatting among the
overalls on the porches of country stores for a whole summer
afternoon, talking to them in their own idiom about nothing
at all" (420). Yet to a degree Faulkner has shown in Gavin
Stevens a contrary approach, not exactly note-taking but de-
achedly intellectual and hyper-analytic, by one who "knew
a good deal less about people than he knew about the law
and about ways of evidence and drawing the right conclu-
sions from what he saw with his legal mind" (*FU*, 140).
"Which," Faulkner added to his university audience, "is not
against education." Neither is it against Gavin Stevens, in
whom the often critical human struggle to reconcile cool
perspective and ardent commitment is significantly dramatized. And with all his loyalty to a powerful imperious "de-

mon," Faulkner himself, in imposing order on his creations, has no doubt experienced a similar struggle for reconciliation.

Nor are the orderings and concentrations of art theoretically rejected by Faulkner; he puts poetry first, and short story "as Chekov did it" second, ahead of "the clumsy method of Mark Twain and Dreiser" (*FU*, 145), and he sees it as a lack that Sherwood Anderson "didn't have a concept of a cosmos in miniature which Balzac and Dickens had" (*FU*, 232). More particularly as to composition, Faulkner is quite committed; asked whether there were not "parts of" *The Sound and the Fury* "that make you feel good enough," he answered, "Well, that's not enough—parts of it are not enough . . . it's either good or it ain't" (*FU*, 62). The containing concept, however, is to be dynamic, not theoretical; asked whether he meant "individual man has prevailed or group man," Faulkner replied, "Man as a part of life," an answer with little comfort in it for organization men, nihilists, sociological new dealers, or literary naturalists, but with contrary emphasis on the verities of a fluid spontaneous personal-social existence. It is thus that Ratliff comes to the fore and is remembered by his creator as "a man who practiced virtue from simple instinct . . . for a practical reason, because it was better," whereas in contrast Gavin is "a more or less artificial man" practicing "what he had been told was a good virtue, apart from his belief in virtues, what he had been told, trained by his respect for education in the old classical sense" (*FU*, 140), another hint that in Gavin Stevens Faulkner has been moved to dramatize the stresses and risks of imbalance in the struggle to equilibrate principle and impulse.

Like any author's single statement under questioning about a character, this is less than the whole truth of the matter, which exists in the work of art entire and nowhere else, and is itself reduced and even falsified by abstraction. Obviously Faulkner as novelist aspires to the same kind of awareness and immediate intuitive horse sense about human beings and their behavior as he shows in Ratliff ("a man who practiced virtue from simple instinct") but quite as surely he knows that the Ratliffs of this world do not write its novels nor even practice in its courts of law. Frequently the dialogues between Ratliff and Gavin Stevens, especially in *The Town*, suggest Faulkner's self-examination, in an attempt to be accountable to his deepest insights and most comprehensive judgments, as they resemble all in Gavin Stevens which transcends Ratliff's view, yet without abstracting them into the undramatic, the fictionally unreal, the non-experiential. Even in person Faulkner leans that way. He called his remarks at the University of Virginia "not the (at the moment of speaking) definite record of the ideas and opinions of a writer on life and literature, including his own work, but . . . rather the self-portrait of a man in motion who also happens to be a writer" (*FU*, viii). The emphasis, as always, is on existence; the aim is constant response to the modes of being and involvement in them, as a personal choice and as the condition of creativity. Nevertheless in courteous response under questioning Faulkner did generalize quite broadly about themes and techniques in his own work and about literature and life. He answered without pretentiousness or pose and also briefly and sometimes almost hesitantly, in distinct contrast to the assurance and zest he seems to have felt in extended fictional elaboration. Like a housed eagle, the grand old artist temporarily held behind the professorial lectern would stretch and fan his great wings slightly with no attempt at flight, knowing an essential difference between realms, habituated as he was to the wider range of the work of art, opening on infinity. Yet in the more artificial academic situation, called on to account definitively for the vast workings of his imagination, Faulkner showed no lack of patience, candor, and geniality, nor gave any sign of an inner conflict. That what he said there is to be fully understood only in the light of his fiction proves him all the more the master.

As in many a dialogue between Ratliff and Gavin Stevens, the elements seem mixed in Faulkner the artist, and his creations show recurrent preponderances, one way or another, all contained within a conceptual and compositional unity. Ratliff personifies the more naturally intuitive and instinctive common man, Stevens the more formally rational cultivated man, yet both men are capable of sensed insights, empathy, judgment, and action, and their powers are not merely complementary to each other's but harmoniously functional within themselves. Gavin's sometimes extravagant theorizings are the hazards a broadly informed and humanely concerned mind cannot refrain from. Occasionally Gavin has for the moment got slightly out of hand, becoming expositor rather than character, as in his summation of the case toward the conclusion of *Intruder in the Dust* (149, 153–56), where ostensibly he is instructing Chick but actually Faulkner is telling the world. Generally, however, Gavin Stevens is not only a fictional figure both credible and narratively contained, he is central, always thematically so and in his frequent acts. Faulkner may allow him a quixotism approaching the ludicrous, may show him in flights of speculation to which Ratliff must say "No" repeatedly and rightly (*T*, 296), and may shape up a quaint figure with such properties as corncob pipe and Heidelberg doctorate, yet Gavin Stevens remains the novelist's surrogate and suffragan, and as such he functions well within the aesthetics of modern fictional illusion. And as usual, illusion vivifies concept. If Gavin Stevens is seen as a real being, a man of like aspirations, fumblings, and persistence, then his central position in Faulkner's scheme of things will be understood, and his relations with Linda in a long series of episodes from her girlhood to her widowhood will take their properly significant place in the whole fable. In particular, if Gavin's motives in aiding Linda's first escape from Jefferson to New York and marriage to Kohl are recognized and remembered, his acquiescence in all that preceded her second departure, after the murder of Flem, will also be seen into, not as collusion or merely supine consent, but as fidelity to a sometimes agonizing involvement, however many technical inconsistencies may be involved. With all his intellectualizing and hairsplitting, Gavin is never a letter-of-the-law attorney, and for all Ratliff's wryness and practicality in the closing episodes of *The Mansion,* he goes along with Stevens, literally and in principle. The consequent transcending of conventions is made possible precisely because of the range of Gavin's mind and the reach of his spirit, just as Ratliff's participation proceeds from the soundness of his instincts.

Faulkner's protagonists are not, however, brash do-gooders, men smugly self-assured as to mission and message. Where angels would fear to tread is perhaps indeterminable, but while Stevens and Ratliff will push on and even rush in if expedition seems required, this is not always foolish, and often it is a saving stroke in the nick of time. Even then no aura of infallibility surrounds these men; they always know it has been a near thing, too, and Ratliff suggests that those who would serve "destiny and fate" (*M,* 370) can do with some "luck, and hope" (*M,* 373–74). In such knowledge and in the face of complexities the Faulknerian protagonist may sometimes hang back, deeply hesitant, unsure of the right course however evident the wrong that should be opposed. The hesitation may show that extreme weariness which comes from bewilderment and a related doubt of personal adequacy, as well as a questioning of personal responsibility. Thus when Gavin is about to meet the troubled Eula at her request (a last meeting, shortly to be followed by her suicide) he thinks, "Why me? . . . Why must it be my problem?" (*T*, 318). Herein again Faulkner represents a modern mood, common and acute, in that challenges from a world embroiled on principle find men loath to be called on for drastic, disinterested commitments, hazarding no end of sacrifice. And as Gavin has asked, "Why me?" so Ratliff at one point had said, "I could do more but I wont. I wont, I tell you!" (*H*, 367). Yet he does do more, repeatedly. Such a flagging of resolution is real and true to common experience; so too is the fact that for some men the halt is only temporary. All this is comprehended in Faulkner's picturing of humane concern as ordeal, and intervention as no less chancy for all its altruism—which adds to the fiction another level of complexity, another degree of tension and dramatic acceleration.

If, as Faulkner said at Charlottesville, Gavin Stevens was "at home" as county attorney and amateur detective but was not "prepared to cope with people who were following their own bent" (*FU*, 140), nevertheless that became precisely what he tried to cope with, and not without success. To attempt what one is not prepared for, that is an old story, and always a significant one, and the confrontation of others who are selfishly following their own bent can be the severest of ordeals for the man of principle, and consequently the very stuff of drama. Finally, not all the pragmatism is left to Ratliff. Gavin Stevens, despite his wasteful digressions on tangents, his too susceptible sympathies, and his lapses into the idealist's melancholy, can pull himself up, take charge, make do, and get the right thing done, or if not that, the best possible thing. From first to last he does help Linda, with a combination of high-mindedness and plain effective good sense. Both times when he gets his face bloodied, by those noisy motorists and aggressive lovers, Manfred and Matt, he remains obviously the better man, and in the first instance, though he certainly "wasn't prepared to cope with" it, he gave his answer to that, for when Charles's father said, "Dont you know you cant fight? You dont know how," Gavin answered, "Can you suggest a better way to learn than the one I just tried?" (*T*, 76).

The idealist proceeding pragmatically, the theorist of verities who does not scorn the securing of half a loaf, is in for many a strain and may be forced into some odd or even superficially inconsistent acts. Gavin Stevens' ordeals are those of his master before him. Faulkner has taken up a most difficult middle ground, where he is subjected to crossfire from every quarter. He is no disciple either of Calvin or of Rousseau; neither has he surrendered his will to determinism of any stripe, economic, social, or philosophical. For all his admiration of Ratliff's instinctive and immediately relevant and effective virtue, Faulkner does not propound a view of mankind's natural goodness, but finds some other men as naturally vicious as Ratliff is virtuous. On the other hand, he is no Manichaean oversimplifier, in any area. Between absolute extremes of good and evil Faulkner finds the imperfect man sometimes rising to a gesture transcending his average self, trying "to be braver than" he is and finds too superiority degenerating into weakness and disgrace. Between the safely strong and the intently wicked he sees the host of the ignorant and the innocent exploited, with a vast waste of human happiness and a defilement of human dignity. The spectacle summons up admiration and disgust, pity and terror, and hope; the issues demand action validating both normal instinct and cultivated judgment. Inevitably to a mind like Faulkner's (or Gavin Stevens') the implicated values will be abstracted and systematized. Inevitably to a nature like Faulkner's (or Ratliff's) the verities will operate as categorical imperatives without being so named, but in the natural gestures of the living and moving man. Still over all is the conceptual, the more than ordinarily comprehensive and imaginative view, consequently more than ordinarily projective. Speculation envisages the chance of breakdown, disruption, and catastrophe, fear becomes the companion of wisdom, and the wearied philosophizing mind thus beset may sometimes long for the serene poise of the natural, as in Ratliff's greater aplomb. Yet whenever the issue becomes acute the more cultivated man is never willing to give up his nervous alertness to possibilities or refuse the urge to pursue the hypotheses they allow—indeed, this is the more "artificial" man's "nature." And from it proceed all manner of things, Gavin's errors and his successes, and their total comprehension in the art of William Faulkner.

In *The Mansion* Gavin is older, and sadder and wiser, but the same man in principle who took up the struggle against Flem in *The Town* and who had exhorted young Chick Mallison of *Intruder in the Dust* never to stop. Later, in *The Mansion,* Charles, the restive law student back at Christmas from Harvard with World War II under way, has lapsed into cynicism, saying that "Man stinks" and that Linda, now attempting to improve the schooling of Jefferson Negroes, should be told her hope of helping people is baseless because "they don't want to be helped any more than they want advice or work. They want cake and excitement, both free," whereupon his uncle Gavin quietly answers, "Why don't you tell her?" and when Charles accepts the rebuke, saying he's sorry, Gavin tells him not to be and adds, "Don't ever waste time regretting errors. Just don't forget them" (230). Coupled with its regard for experience as guide to immediate action and determinant of values to be aimed at, Gavin's "Don't ever waste time regretting errors" also pointedly answers Eula's words of years before, "Dont waste time expecting" (*T*, 94), and separates Gavin not only from that doomed woman so tangled in nature's and certain men's snares, but from all whose surrender to circumstance denies self-determination and makes them the hopeless pawns of those like the Snopeses, whose aggressive and acquisitive expectations draw a terrible efficiency from specialization. Gavin nearing sixty is still the man of probity and compassion confronting resurgent evil, recognizing faults in himself and those he has most regard for, and by coupling the denial of "any morals" with the practice of doing "the best" possible, he asserts fallible man's indomitable idealism, the essence indeed of the tragic sense of life, "human unsuccess" to be sung "in a rapture of distress," and thus "In the deserts of the heart" to "Let the healing fountain start."

As in classic tragedy, so here in the trilogy the bold presence of conflicting passions and unlawful violence should not obscure the high conceptual level of the action. Some reviewers professed themselves shocked by Gavin Stevens' concluding activities in *The Mansion*, stressing his collusion with Linda, as accessory before and after the fact of Flem's murder. This lawyer's conduct, however, is not always to be judged so legalistically. When Gavin has said, "There aren't any morals," he is specifically answering Ratliff's humorous review of Flem's whole acquisitive life as having resulted simply in a return of the mansion to De Spain relatives who probably do not want it. Ratliff's wry conclusion that "maybe there's even a moral in it somewhere, if you jest knowed where to look," plays upon the notion of "morals" as platitude—the Aesopian q.e.d., an assumption of simple detectable cause and effect conventionalized into a precise invariable rule—which is what Gavin is denying. When after saying, in this context, that "There aren't any morals," Gavin adds that "People just do the best they can," he is asserting that there is something like morality, in the principled attempt to make the humanly preferable prevail, to whatever attainable degree. As usual, Gavin Stevens is confronting reality in its complexity, and attempting to adapt tactics without surrender of strategic principle. One thing he refuses to do is to lapse into the cynicism and indifference which are easy refuges for some who find the letter of the law, either civil or canon, to be inoperative. Instead he has gone on always just doing the best he can, in the midst of confusions and contradictions, but by the light of a disinterested and sympathetic concern for others. It is scarcely just, then, for critics to pick technical fault with his actions in the closing pages of *The Mansion* or to suggest, as did Anthony West in *The New Yorker*,[2] that Gavin Stevens, "nice chap that he is," has declined "through silliness into inanity."

And Linda is wrong when just before her departure she tells Gavin, "You have had nothing" (*M*, 424). Whatever his life has been it has not been empty. The quixotic life never is, and he touches that in his immediate response:

He knew exactly what she meant: her mother first, then her; that he had offered the devotion twice and got back for it nothing but the privilege of being obsessed, bewitched, besotted if you like; Ratliff certainly would have said besotted (*M*, 424–25).

This more than nothing transcends these names for it, is more than obsession and bewitchment, and much more than

[2] December 5, 1959, pp. 230, 232.

besottedness; it is a fabric of experience which he suggests to himself in the successively rejected replies he could have written on the deaf Linda's tablet: "I have everything. You trusted me. You chose to let me find you murdered your so-called father rather than tell me a lie," or "I have everything. Haven't I just finished being accessory before a murder." Instead his written reply is "We have had everything" (*M*, 425), and it would seem to mean they have carried through together, he has supported Linda in every issue, she has valued his support, and he has known it valued. It goes beyond what Ratliff has truly enough remarked in *The Town*: "And being the next-best to Paris is jest a next-best too, but it aint no bad next-best to be. Not ever body had Helen, but then not ever body lost her neither" (101).

Having in the sense of possession was not what Gavin was after; had it been, he could have taken what Eula and then Linda proposed. During the early years of the war Eula, tied to the impotent Flem and tangled in her known affair with De Spain, was understandably fatalistic about all such relations, but Linda, having known love with Barton Kohl, and continuing in a much closer, more extended relation with Gavin than her mother's, and developing a much more complex feeling for him, comes to realize why what she pathetically offered could not be right for either of them. Beyond that, Gavin's finally marrying has seemed to accord with Linda's analytical advice (*M*, 252) that he "just stop resisting the idea," but this is because she, like all the rest except finally Charles, knows nothing of Gavin's long, secret, obstructed devotion to Melisandre. Linda's desire, however, that Gavin "have that too" (*M*, 252), as she had known it with Kohl, is attained. "Nobody must never have had that once," Linda has said (*M*, 241), and has explained how much more than just the sexual relation she means, the rest of it, the little things: it's this pillow still holding the shape of the head, this necktie still holding the shape of the throat that took it off last night even just hanging empty on a bedpost, even the empty shoes on the floor still sit with the right one turned out a little like his feet were still in them and even still walking the way he walked (*M*, 251).

Of all such things in his own marriage Gavin never speaks, nor does Faulkner for him, but this reticence makes lesser detail the more implicative. Through the years when Melisandre was married to Harriss, then was a widow living abroad, and then returned with her grown children and Gualdres the supposed suitor, Gavin waited in a significant silence that the young Charles of "Knight's Gambit" had noticed (155, 160, 164), for what Gavin persistently resisted was not the idea of marriage but fate's obstacles to his choice, and these are overcome at last. Gavin's match is apparently a success; when he phones his wife that he will not be home to dinner, and this because of involvement with the Flem-Mink-Linda problem, they spar in the manner of people who are charmed with each other, and he humorously says, "How can I resist togetherness if you wont fight back?" (*M*, 383). In such a marriage Gavin can remain as much concerned with Linda as ever, considering the nature of his solicitude. Thus what Gavin writes at last on the deaf woman's tablet just before her departure—"We have had everything" —is profoundly true; humanly involved in the same baffling events, they have been each other's care, have met on the high ground of devotion unequivocally expressive of themselves, and have accepted each other's influence as a grace, even in ordeal. Generous sentiment has run deep and constant between them. Consequently Gavin must reject as inadequate first *I have had* this and then *I have had* that, and when he changes to *We have had*, he can add *everything*, and mean it.

Faulkner means it too. Unlike many of his contemporaries, he is not afraid of sentiment; he neither flinches from it nor neutralizes its force by an attenuated or debased representation. This is one of the reasons his work seems so powerful by comparison with that of his contemporaries, since in storytelling it is sentiment primarily which underlies dynamic motivation and the most crucial drama. Some may allege that Gavin Stevens has been fitted out with everything but a Rosinante and a white plume; on the other hand, it is never claimed nor implied for him, even in his occasional successes, that his strength is as the strength of ten, nor is he made wholly pure of heart. But probity he does have, and aspiration, benevolence, and fidelity. For all his eccentricities there is a harmony about Gavin Stevens. Tempered by fear (that fear which is the beginning of wisdom and which accompanies knowledge of good and evil), he does indeed "live by admiration, hope, and love." And the strong strain of sentiment in him—almost a constant in his consciousness and a determinant in all his acts—makes him, this side sentimentality, a rare modern instance, a rounded man. He seems heir of several streams out of these last three centuries which their accelerated crowding has made like ages; he is rational, and intuitive, and engaged, one who, therefore, is because he thinks, and feels, and acts.

Neglect to recognize and value this full characterization of a major figure in its thematic and dramatic aspects is a failure to read Faulkner; indeed, it misses the main point of the Snopes trilogy. This massive work manifests the aesthetic trait of unity in variety and will be violated by any piecemeal relishing. While the heterogeneous cast and their multiform actions furnish the variety, issue is the unifying factor, and it is in this single steady light that the opulent characterization is made plain. While Gavin Stevens' quixotic acts and thoughts, together with Ratliff's ironies, are in themselves variations, all this is differently motivated and toward an opposite order of values from that of Snopesism, so that these extremes balance each other on the pivot of the ethical. The subtle counterpoint of *The Wild Palms* was sacrificed to commerce, to get a couple of books typographically out of one, but the Snopes saga is too well knit for that, and those who praise the Mink Snopes portion as though it were self-sustained and extractable are perhaps only failing to sense how much their response draws on the rest of the trilogy, through a reader's marginal consciousness of the relevant, and particularly as to the tangential illumination projected across the action by Stevens, Ratliff, and Charles. Above all, it can be seen that Gavin Stevens as quixotic champion, a man of refined feeling and imperative sentiment, is also judicious and decisively active, a man whose alertness to fact is the very opposite of sentimentality, and whose idealism does not scorn the serviceably practical. The nature of his involvement with mankind, however, can be fully realized only in the thematic terms of ethical issue, humanely defined and asserted as an act of personal responsibility. So viewed, Gavin will emerge as a character most credible and empathetically engaging, his eccentricities wrung from him by ordeal and his extravagances the gestures of one ready at any time to go all out in the disinterestedly approximated right direction.

Admittedly Gavin's admiration of women will seem odd to many moderns in its tincture of romantic awe that sometimes tapers off into a fatalistic view of the separate natures of men and women and of woman's impact. (But other contemporaries have noted some such difference; it has been variously expressed by Conrad, Shaw, and Thurber.) Woman "fits herself to no environment" but "just by breathing, just by the mere presence of that fragile and delicate flesh, warps and wrenches milieu itself" (*T*, 284), Gavin Stevens thinks, believing also what Eula once told him (*T*, 226), that "women dont really care about facts just so they fit" (*T*, 358), whereas men value facts, however destructive, above the fitting, a view supported by Ratliff, that bachelor so widely acquainted in the county, who opined that women "dont need reasons . . . dont function from reasons but from necessities that couldn't nobody help nohow and that dont nobody but a fool man want to help in the second place" (*M*, 117). Eula herself has voiced this opinion of her own sex:

"Women arent interested in poets' dreams. They are interested in facts. It doesn't even matter whether the facts are true or not, as long as they match the other facts without leaving a rough seam" (*T*, 226).

Gavin, however, credits the poets and in so doing uses the same terminology, saying that

"poets . . . are not really interested in facts: only in truth: which is why the truth they speak is so true that even those who hate poets by simple natural instinct are exalted and terrified by it" (*T*, 88).

Charles Mallison defines more particularly something akin to what Eula had implied by "It doesn't even matter whether the facts are true or not" (*T*, 226). After observing some of his mother's typical behavior, he says that

women are marvellous. They stroll perfectly bland and serene through a fact that the men have been bloodying their heads against for years; whereupon you find that the fact not only wasn't important, it wasn't really there (*M*, 215).

Ratliff, with further regard to this question of women's attitudes toward facts, dreams, and truth, sees an often insuperable block to communication between the sexes, and he

finds an inhibiting difference in women's more deeply instinctive life. This he himself seems to have absorbed intuitively by long observation, and when Gavin admits he
doesn't "know anything about women" and asks Ratliff, "So
would you mind telling me how the hell you learned?" Ratliff answers typically, "Maybe by listening," and when Gavin
says, "So I didn't listen to the right ones," Ratliff replies, "Or
the wrong ones neither . . . because by that time you were
already talking again" (*T*, 229). The problem, however, as
Ratliff sees it, is not just that men don't listen, it is also that
women aren't fully cognizant of their own natures, or at
least are unable to define themselves to others, especially to
men. Stevens never understood Eula, Ratliff says, and never
realized she understood him "because she never had no way
of telling him because she didn't know herself how she done
it." Generalizing, Ratliff goes on that "women learn at about
two or three years old and then forget it, the knowledge
about their-selves that a man stumbles on by accident forty-
odd years later" (*T*, 100, 101).

Nothing could be more characteristic of Faulkner than
this jangle of somewhat coincident but still dissident opinion
from these three, and its special characterizing of Gavin, as
one whose instincts are not simple but who accepts both ex-
altation and terror (*T*, 88) as part of a mature humane man's
natural responses to reality. Eula (like Linda after her) typi-
fies the feminine in two ways—by her physical allure and by
the fate it brings upon her. When biological and social facts
tend to enclose such women early and irredeemably, thereafter they must make do, expediently, as Eula does in her
marriage to Flem and her affair with De Spain. So does
Linda, returning to her not-father's mansion and seeing her
mother revenged through Mink's revenge, and meanwhile in
widowhood and deafness depending on Gavin in a relation-

ship that can never evolve into definition and permanence. What Ratliff understands is this enforced expediency in many women's lives; he has often seen it in operation and knows it as the only course of action open to such women, and their way of survival; hence in *The Hamlet* he knows his aid to Mink's wife and children after Mink is jailed is only an amelioration, on the assumption that no radical remedy is possible. But Gavin is addicted to that poets' particular dream named truth, and for him it inheres in an ideal, which he would make effective for women, something beyond the bare necessities they secure for themselves by their brave fatalistic expediency. What Ratliff observes Gavin makes the basis of idealistic attitude and drastic action; thus his chivalry is more than sentimentalized sexuality, it acknowledges a belief in women's genius for making things fit, however arbitrarily, and for making them be fit, as may be, with a spirit that lifts endurance above mere stoic necessity and gives it human grace—a quality Faulkner has found variously expressed in a variety of women. Whatever the relative truth of this belief, even when Gavin's chivalry veers toward the quixotic it is to be seen as more than a mere romanticizing by himself or by Faulkner.

Indeed, in the recognition of woman as the mysterious exalted object of love the other folk of Yoknapatawpha County are not altogether remiss. Aspects of the sexual are naturally targets of their bucolic wit, and Ratliff knows his audience when he counts months and remarks that Eula's baby just brought back from Texas "aint hardly big enough to be chewing tobacco yet, I reckon." Such talk stops there, though, when Bookwright tells him, "It wouldn't chew. It's a girl" (*H*, 302). With that word the story opens into what is to be another cycle, extending throughout the rest of the trilogy, Linda's emergence into womanhood, a course in no way resembling her mother's except by severity of fate, and a consequent pathos similarly acknowledged by observers, and epitomized in Charles's repeated comment, "Lost" (*M*, 219). Linda's mother, Eula Varner, at first just the indolent adolescent but soon the center of a swarm of young men in buggies, was sensed as one of earth's rare daughters of "the spendthrift Olympian ejaculation," and becomes with her arranged marriage to Flem the object of "a word . . . born of envy and old deathless regret, murmured from cabin to cabin above the washing pots and the sewing, from wagon to horseman in roads" (*H*, 169). After her return as Mrs. Snopes she is seen in moving aspect when the men go to her father's house to summon Varner for the injured Armstid and she comes to the window in the moonlight:

She did not lean out, she merely stood there, full in the moon, apparently blank-eyed or certainly not looking downward at them —the heavy gold hair, the mask not tragic and perhaps not even doomed: just damned, the strong faint lift of breasts beneath marblelike fall of the garment; to those below what Brunhilde, what Rhinemaiden on what spurious river-rock of papier-mache, what Helen returned to what topless and shoddy Argos, waiting for no one (*H*, 349–50).

Faulkner has played on this distinction earlier; Ratliff has seen young Mrs. Snopes on her return passing by with her mother in the surrey, "the beautiful face . . . in profile, calm, oblivious, incurious . . . not a tragic face: it was just damned" (*H*, 304). Doom as tragedy implies a chosen action, a flaw but a freedom too. To be "just damned" is the predestination Eula must accept more passively, as is suggested by her posture and gaze—at the window "apparently blank-eyed, certainly not looking downward at them"—in the surrey "in profile, calm, oblivious, incurious."

From such damnation she turns to an affair with Manfred

de Spain, in that expediency which is the only path of assertion for a woman caught by circumstance. Acting instinctively, she arrives at a certain fitness, even though it does not comprise all the facts of her situation. Ratliff see it in all its simplicity:

All the understanding one another they needed was you might say for both of them to agree on when and where next and jest how long away it would have to be. But apart from that, they never no more needed to waste time understanding one another than sun and water did to make rain. They never no more needed to be drawed together than sun and water needed to be (*T*, 99–100).

At the Cotillion Ball her dancing with Manfred intimidates "the little puny people fallen back speechless and aghast" before "that splendor, that splendid unshame" (*T*, 75). Then after "eighteen years" of it the town, out of accumulated jealousy male and female, is ready to see retribution upon the pair and a symbolic wiping out of the sin itself—"that splendor must not only not exist, it must never have existed" (*T*, 308). So, caught in circumstance again after so many years, beset by contradictory facts, Eula finds once more what fitness she can, choosing expediently, as less shocking to her daughter, to commit suicide rather than run off with De Spain.

Hence Gavin's tears, for the pathos of it, the inadequacy of that degree of realization, the partial fitting together of the disparate, which is all that is available to such predestinately damned women. Linda's desolateness after the loss of mother and husband and the onset of deafness, and her strained association with Flem in the only thing like a home she has to return to, are similarly harsh facts, making her pitiably appealing, which Charles sees as well as Gavin. Moreover, her misfortunes (like her mother's) thematically involve "Snopesism," but in global as well as local terms. Gavin is not tilting at a windmill; he is struggling hand to hand with a very present evil. Behind intervention is attitude, infused with sentiment, and his attentions to this lonely injured young woman, like his other acts, spring out of reflective concern with values, in a serious engagement with reality.

Gavin Stevens' chivalry, then, is fundamental, in that he is protagonist of the ethic which is most explicit in putting women and children first but which applies in defense of all common human rights and of any decency, civility, and gentility conservative of such rights. Gavin's quixotism is not an aberration but simply an extravagance, a generous expenditure in the direction of the humane, setting the perhaps possible above the probable, and if it is cavalier, it is gallantly so, sensing honor vitally as something beyond position and assumption, to be lived up to in progressive conduct. Such a pursuit, as Gavin finds repeatedly, must face up to the always difficult transit from theory to practice, and must go the tortuous second mile in the spirit of the law, beyond its masking letter. And for Gavin Stevens too, as for others, the issue is to be joined at last on personal and private grounds, in the solitary subjective struggle against despair, to maintain firmness of mind while avoiding hardness of heart. This is the essence of Gavin Stevens' story, and in this light whatever may seem paradoxical in his being and conduct proceeds from the inclusive paradox of idealism itself:

> to hope till Hope creates
> From its own wreck the thing it contemplates.

And since Gavin Stevens' gallantry, however quixotic at moments and in detail, is in the main a humanely perceptive man's responsible involvement with mankind and a rigorous confrontation of reality, Faulkner's full careful delineation of this as motion, as process in all its complexity, is an equally responsible realism, comprehensively conceived, scrupulously executed.

6

"running in a wild lateral turmoil among the unrecovered leaves"

At this point arises perhaps the most crucial issue in evaluating Faulkner's achievement. Faulkner obviously subscribes to that first item of the serious artist's credo voiced by Conrad as the "conviction that the world, the temporal world, rests on a few very simple ideas; so simple that they must be as old as the hills." Conrad cites as one of the most notable "the idea of Fidelity."[1] Similarly Faulkner has mentioned certain "verities"—notably "courage, honor, pride compassion, pity"—which are also, in Conrad's sense, "very simple ideas," and also related to conduct. How then, if the principles of conduct are explicit, pertinent, and literally basic, can so much complication enter in, and more especially, so much confusion and distortion? Still more particularly, how is it that grotesqueness not only pervades the behavior of the unprincipled and consequently of their vic-

[1] "A Familiar Preface," *A Personal Record* (New York: Doubleday, Page and Co., 1925), p. xxi.

138

tims but colors actions by protagonists of the verities? Some criticism, especially before Faulkner became "famous," has labeled the grotesqueness in his works slapdash or even purposely sensational, but it deserves a closer view than that, being so pervasive and apparently intentional.

That Faulkner's work abounds in the grotesque brooded upon until it deepens into a kind of Gothic darkness is undeniable. Characters as various as Mink and Linda, too severely beset and hurt, are twisted thereby into almost inhumanly strange attitudes. In Flem and in such lesser kinfolk as Montgomery Ward, I. O. Snopes, and Lump, the grotesque more or less eclipses the human. When such deformation is traced to its source, it seems to rise out of nature itself, grossly atavistic and unamenable, as in all the Snopeses, the life process at its most alarmingly mutative, until to judge the species by the sport would be to see man as Stevenson's "monster of the agglutinated dust." But Faulkner does not imply even any such momentary surrender to a sense of overwhelming corruption. While the Snopeses confirm Mrs. Moore's vision at Malabar of something "snub-nosed, incapable of generosity—the undying worm itself," many of Faulkner's commoners, like his genuine aristocrats, are sound and honorable, and for him the cosmos is still the stage of a running battle between darkness and light, neither of them illusory. Yet in such a closely matched fight, there is much mutually impelled awkwardness. If Faulkner's wrongdoers are particularly distorted by their obsessions, those who resist them are forced to complementary extremes. The resultant grotesqueness throughout Faulkner's fiction can scarcely be read, however, as mere expedient melodrama. It is rather the shadowing-forth of a realistic world view, and this facing of overbalancing and erosive struggles in no way invalidates conviction formed and held against vulgarities, indifference, inequities, and aggression.

The question of extravagance in its relation to realism is apparently a recurrent one. A century ago Victorian theorists of fiction (recently summarized in Richard Stang's able study)[2] were attempting a distinction between the two tendencies represented by Thackeray and Dickens, with special reference to Dickens's more liberal practice. Samuel Lucas, editor of *Once A Week* and writer for *The Times*, described the two schools as those who, like Thackeray, presented the work "phenomenally" or those like Dickens who drew more upon "inner consciousness"; and Lucas defended Meredith as of the second group, whom he called "humourists." The argument, suggestive of much that was to follow in fiction, sets over against "manners" the expression of "modes of thought," of which fictitious characters are "symbols and shadows," with the consequence that any such work must be judged in view of "the plan and object of its creation" (187). A similar distinction, this time in defense of *Wuthering Heights* and *Jane Eyre*, was advanced by Sydney Dobell, who termed writers of Thackeray's kind "perceptive," sketchers of "portraits" from "outward experience," whereas those like Dickens were "ideal," drawing "from within" for the amplification of attitude; and Dobell values these "ideal" writers above the merely "perceptive" (188).

Both tendencies were approved by David Masson, who named them the "real" and the "ideal," likewise finding these categories typified in Thackeray and Dickens (189). While not depreciating Thackeray, Masson defended Dickens and his "world projected imaginatively beyond the real one" (190), in which observed oddity is treated with further

[2] *The Theory of the Novel in England: 1850–1870* (London: Routledge & Kegan Paul, 1959).

exaggeration. The fictionist's "ideal" practice had precedent, Masson found, in Greek tragedy, with its transcendence of the commonplace and its implication of the archetypal, "large, superb, and unapproachable" (190). Shakespeare too he cited as of the "ideal" tendency in representing "grand hyperbolic beings" . . . "humanity caught, as it were, and kept permanent in its highest and extremest mood" (190). In this light Masson claimed for the novel the right to aspire to the quality of "prose Epic" (86), the work of "prose poets" . . . "men avoiding nothing as too fantastic for their element, but free and daring in it as the verse-poet is in his" (88).

Whatever the terminology, the issue was real. It remains unsettled, and whoever pays attention can still take his choice, but at least two points should be noted in these various nineteenth-century defenses of Dickens, the Brontës, and Meredith. First, most simply, is the claim for the novel of rights and privileges beyond the plain ground of a commonplace realism. Prose fiction need not be prosaic; it may appropriate almost every one of the poet's devices. In this connection Faulkner himself has said he thinks "any writer is better off if he looks on himself . . . primarily as a poet" (*FU*, 145). More broadly, in one way or another these Victorian critics were promulgating that most solidly liberal view which makes precedents dynamic, and gains scope by citing previously established values to emancipate practice from the bonds of an overweening current fashion. Their example suggests a similarly discriminating exemption of Faulkner from disapproval for differing from the sort of "objectivity" made virtually *de rigueur* in the name of Hemingway, though seldom with full understanding of the alleged example.

Yet with the word objective, as with all those other Victorian abstractions—subjective, phenomenal, ideal, real, and even perceptive—there is the risk of implying a bifurcation false to the nature of genuine works of narrative art. The actions of a novel must be comprised in an action; mimesis must be complemented by harmonia. The humourist, whether his mode be that of Jonson, Sterne, or Lamb, identifies humours in the light of norms. The word humour itself, turned to verb, is made to imply an indulgence, an allowance extended under law, though not *ex officio* but leniently. Latitudes granted his fellows by the humourist imply not looseness but largeness of principle, which is made relative enough to admit a mysteriously complex reality. Nor does concern with humours confine itself to the ludicrous to the exclusion of pathos, and that complexion is possible because eccentricity, when seen literally as such, is known to have not only its quaintness but its cost, to itself and often to others.

Herein also Faulkner's work (for clarification of critical principles and to its credit besides) should be distinguished from a more predominant contemporary trend, that of treating aberration as mere behavioral phenomenon, occurrence equated to no humanistic norm, in a naturalism chary of value judgments, and consequently as little amusing or pathetic, and as far from the tragicomic, as a caseworker's report. Basically this sort of naturalism is a leveling off of the Thackeray-Dickens, phenomenal-ideal tendencies in a way to cancel out the particular merits of each. And it is a neglect of the imaginative nature of art and a misunderstanding of realism itself to see Dickens's or Shakespeare's or Faulkner's exaggerations as unreal and escapist, their fantasy as a supposed substitution for the veracious. The fantastic is instead a part of the rhetoric of emphasis, and each grotesquerie is to be judged not for correspondence to isolated fact but for its service to imaginative expression.

Strictest accordance with reality is rather to be sought in the concept; in this sort of entity Flem Snopes will not seem a too drastically imagined toad in the real garden of Yoknapatawpha County, which has for its literalness quite as adequate a cast of characters as Eden.

There are many aspects and degrees of the grotesque in all of Faulkner's work, but especially in the Snopes trilogy, where it abets a variety in unity that enhances composition and illuminates theme. There is as a primary element the simple grotesque of oddly fanciful expression, typifying a vitality which may color any incidental exchange, as when Bookwright in *The Hamlet*, warning Ratliff about Snopes acquisitiveness, says, "If I was you I would go out there nekkid in the first place. Then you wont notice the cold coming back" (82), or when, after young Gowan in *The Town* has made what could be taken as a precocious remark about women, Charles Mallison's father, always a high, wide, and handsome talker, says, "Hold him while I look at his teeth again. You told me he wasn't but thirteen" (56). And Chick the high school student, handing Gavin another note from Linda, makes an early try at the extravagant-figurative, saying, "It seems to be stuck . . . . The record . . . . This is the same tune it was playing before, aint it? Just backward this time" (*T*, 215).

Charles grown continues to develop the vein, with his more matured and wryer interest in his uncle's doings, and while he is in Cambridge after Linda Kohl's return to Jefferson, he muses with collegiate ribaldry about wiring Ratliff to ask,

Is it rosa yet or still just sub, assuming you assume the same assumption they teach us up here at Harvard that once you get the clothes off those tall up-and-down women you find out they aint all that up-and-down at all (*M*, 205).

He goes on to fancy grotesquely that perhaps the delay is for his sake, to wait until Christmas,

> not to interrupt my education by an emergency call but for the season of peace and good will to produce me available to tote the ring or bouquet or whatever it is (*M*, 205–6).

And later, with "still no wedding bells," Charles puts it to himself, and so to the reader, that since deafened Linda's private voice lessons with Gavin were still going on, "maybe she felt that the Yes would not be dulcet enough yet to be legal" (*M*, 209). Curiously fanciful and blunt as these grotesque phrasings are, they suggest awareness of almost inscrutable complexities, and a far from simple response to them. Thereby they dramatize more fully the spectator-narrator, according his tone and gesture to the report, and often conveying his view most revealingly by these tinges of the grotesque, in which wryness can be the paradoxical index of a deep concern. Here as in much modern literature and painting, it is at the very point of crudity and apparent obviousness that significant subtleties are overlaid.

And it is in this same mode that grotesqueness often enters into Faulkner's own descriptive imagery. In *The Hamlet* is this glimpse of Eula as indolent child borne by a servant with her mother going visiting:

> Mrs. Varner in her Sunday dress and shawl, followed by the negro man staggering slightly beneath his long, dangling, already indisputably female burden like a bizarre and chaperoned Sabine rape (108).

A different kind of effect, but similarly intensified and almost surrealistically imaginative, is in the envisaging of a figure at a high school commencement, "in the hot stiff brand-new serge suit, to walk sweating through the soundless agony of the cut flowers" (*T*, 144), or in that seizure and dream-like exaggeration of the instant which stresses the illusory, as when to Ratliff, passing the cotton fields, "the pickers, arrested in stooping attitudes, seemed fixed amid the constant surf of bursting bolls like piles in surf, the long, partly-filled sacks streaming away behind them like rigid frozen flags" (*H*, 170). With Faulkner such arrestment, however, is never merely picturesque, never an incidental flourish or narrative padding; the grotesque, even in description, always carries the thematic overtones and, as Conrad put it in his most famous preface, "creates the moral, the emotional atmosphere of the place and time." "I read some of Dickens every year," Faulkner significantly has said (*FU*, 50), and he also declared it "the artist's prerogative . . . to emphasize, to underline, to blow up facts, distort facts in order to state a truth," adding that "there's probably no tribe of Snopeses in Mississippi or anywhere else outside of my own apocrypha . . . they were simply over-emphasized, burlesqued if you like, which is what Mr. Dickens spent a lot of his time doing, for a valid to him and to me reason, which was to tell a story in an amusing, dramatic, tragic, or comical way" (*FU*, 282). This indicates that the grotesque in Faulkner's fiction is neither a carelessness nor a weakness, not a loss of focus and control but a comprehensively employed device, resorted to with some sense of artistic precedent.

Even without this report, indeed, such direct influence of Dickens is apparent in Faulkner's work, as in that of James and, more directly, Conrad. But Faulkner's modern use of the grotesque, further advanced and specially developed, goes beyond that of all such eminent predecessors. Though in two quite separate ways and at very different levels, Dickens and James both employed extravagant distortion most typically within an omniscient point of view, whereas

in Faulkner the perception of the grotesque, though sometimes defined in the author's own terms, is quite often delegated to the characters, whose voicing of it usually attains
the level of irony as a trait of character, entering into the
tone of the whole passage. Dickens's comic folk, extremely
caricatured, are generally "flat" as Forster defines the term—
each "in his humour" and simply that—and their qualities
are comprised in Dickens's own boldly phrased vignettes or
else in set conversation which while voluble is but the constant mirror of a child-like mind, innocently obsessed.
Dickens continues the English enthusiasm for idiosyncrasy
of which Lamb was the foremost apologist; both, like their
predecessors, will count the streaks of an eccentricity for its
own sake, in sheer pleasure that a man should be so mark-
edly himself; and in this mode the grotesque may become
a reassuring index of free and easy self-determination, which
not even a Dickens villain can grind down. Mark Twain's
incidental exaggerations assert the same sort of personal
independence, in grotesqueries defiant of reason itself, but
thereby also parodying the confining stereotypes into which
systematic purpose can deteriorate; Mark's play is more than
simply playful, with the bizarre as satire, rooted in rational
grounds. But while in Dickens (as in Lamb and the "character" writers) the eccentric often is epitomized for its own
sake as static instance, more recent fiction is more closely
and consistently thematic. Here too James went beyond
Dickens; James uses eccentric personality and conduct,
highlighted into the grotesque, for a veiled but intent criticism of life, as well as for the pointing up of dramatic
conflict. Quite frequently in James the grotesque (which in
Dickens so often accompanies simple virtue and invincible
golden-heartedness) points to insensitivity—intellectual,
aesthetic, social, and moral.

In Faulkner's protagonists the perception of another's insensitivity and ruthlessness can stimulate conversely their most extravagant phrasings, which, while often broadly comic on the surface, also serve to intensify the pathos of the victimized, through that personal undertone of the sardonic which the grotesque so frequently sounds. In James's works critical judgments of behavior, at their most exaggeratedly and even grotesquely expressed, are often delivered by the author himself or in the true Jamesian tone delegated unmodified. In that remarkable story so brimming with gusto and saturated with tragicomedy, "The Death of the Lion," he has specifically reserved the privilege of discrimination by using first-person narrative, as the journalist who goes to interview the distinguished author, Neil Paraday, and in the ensuing intimacy sees him collected as a house-party item by Mrs. Weeks Wimbush, "wife of the boundless brewer and proprietress of the universal menagerie," who considers Paraday "a creature of almost heraldic oddity"[3] but then neglects him for the really odd company of the avidly social she has assembled, including a Princess, "a massive lady with the organization of an athlete and the confusion of tongues of a *valet de place*."[4] Sometimes James dominantly creates the ironic grotesque by a pomp of circumlocution; in "The Pupil," after describing Mr. Moreen's white moustache and ribbon of a foreign order in his buttonhole as marks of "a man of the world," he writes that "Ulick, the firstborn, was in visible training for the same profession—under the disadvantage as yet, however, of a buttonhole but feebly floral and a moustache with no pretensions to type."[5] There is no doubt as to who for the

[3] *The Lesson of the Master*, Vol. XV (New York: Scribner, 1922), p. 123.
[4] *The Lesson of the Master*, Vol. XV, p. 141.
[5] *What Maisie Knew*, Vol. XI (New York: Scribner, 1922), p. 517.

moment is in charge here, though the perception is also the tutor's, as the central intelligence.

Conrad, working in the great tradition advanced by James in English fiction but moving further with the theory of illusion, will sometimes grant grotesqueness of expression to a character to whom the telling of the story has been wholly or at least largely delegated. For instance, in "Heart of Darkness"—a story Faulkner, like many another writer, has cited as a favorite (*FU*, 150)—Marlow encounters a whole gallery of eccentrics and describes them as such. Briefly but of unforgettable aspect and with thematic resonance, there is the secretary in the Belgian home office, "whitehaired," beckoning with "a skinny forefinger," "full of desolation and sympathy" as Marlow signs his contract, and mentioning the required medical examination "with an air of taking an immense part in all my sorrows" (56, 57). There is the patched-clothed young Russian in the Congo jungle, "in motley, as though he had absconded from a troupe of mimes, enthusiastic, fabulous" (126). This undiscriminating admirer of Kurtz at his worst becomes a point of reference in the fable, as the complete adventurer and vivacious amoralist, in his "particoloured rags," with "no features to speak of" and "smiles and frowns chasing each other over that open countenance like sunshine and shadow on a windswept plain" (122). Marlow does not envy him his "unmeditated" devotion (127) to Kurtz, and sees him bemused by ruthless power and uncritically submissive to it— the kind of surrender to colonialism's expediencies which Marlow on every step along the way has refused to make— and thus each stroke of grotesque imagery outlining the young Russian, each infatuated speech of his enhances the ethical theme and further certifies the troubled but uncompromising Marlow as its dependable spokesman.

Here Marlow is a primary actor in the drama, but indeed it is as a fabulizer that he most strongly emerges as *persona*, and so too it is with Gavin Stevens, Ratliff, and Charles Mallison. Whereas Dickens stereotypes the grotesque, and uses it incidentally or at most for a sort of comic relief or static virtue or villainy, Conrad characteristically abstracts and themes the grotesque, although picturesquely too. Advancing beyond James and far beyond Dickens (in spite of certain close resemblances, especially in the treatment of minor characters), Conrad foreshadows Faulkner's fuller incorporation of the grotesque into the dramatic flow, and often subjectively, putting it within the consciousness of a character, and within a passing moment and circumstance of the story. Such a practice becomes part of that firm recasting of conventional techniques which gives Faulkner's creations organic strength. Whereas Ratliff in the original "Spotted Horses" yarn, like Marlow in most of "Heart of Darkness," is the continuous narrator, with a sort of authorial command and presence, in the Snopes trilogy the variations of narrative technique have something of the shiftings of cinematic photography, not only in point of view but in focus and depth, and the grotesque especially as exaggeration or distortion recurs transiently, an aspect of the moment but relevant in the continuum. Faulkner's conceived work of art is furnished forth by the concepts of his several characters, in whom awareness of the grotesque is sharply expressive of insights contributive to theme.

Thus Faulkner can let his protagonists share the power of grotesque imaging and imagining, as when Charles Mallison, describing the inseparable half-breed children Byron Snopes sends Flem from Texas, says, "It was always all four of them, as if when the medicine man or whoever it was separated each succeeding one from the mother, he just attached the severed cord to the next senior child" (*T*, 361). A more extended and diffuse grotesquerie is that strange Southern mélange of violence and punctilio in *The Town* when De Spain repeatedly drives past with the cut-out open to taunt Gavin and young Gowan sets the rake-head that punctures the tire, whereupon Gavin's sister, mistress of the house, sends out a servant in a white jacket with coffee, cream, and sugar on a tray for De Spain (*T*, 62). To read these exaggerated gestures as idle farce would be to miss their suggestion of feeling so heightened and complicated that it must be expressed as something other than itself, through every means from swagger to hyper-formality, and all of it hence grotesque. Charles Mallison, reconstructing some of these events from hearsay, including the flood of corsages and the fist fight between Gavin and Manfred, sees that the boisterousness and even the violence could have been products of otherwise inexpressible stress. So, he thinks, it must have been with Eula Varner Snopes's lover:

I reckon there was a second when even he said Hold on here; have I maybe blundered into something not just purer than me but even braver than me, braver and tougher than me because it is purer than me, cleaner than me? (*T*, 74)

Continuing such speculation, Charles reflects:

And when I was old enough, fourteen or fifteen or sixteen, I knew what Gowan had seen without knowing what he was seeing: that second when Mr de Spain felt astonishment, amazement and unbelief and terror too at himself because of what he found himself doing without even knowing he was going to—dancing like that with Mrs Snopes to take revenge on Uncle Gavin for having frightened him, Mr de Spain, enough to make him play the sophomore tricks like the cut-out and the rake-head and the used rubber thing in a corsage; frightened at himself at finding out that he couldn't possibly be only what he had thought for all those years he was, if he could find himself in a condition capable of playing tricks like that (*T*, 74–75).

Thus is the grotesque in conduct incorporated into composition and made expressive of concept.

Often in the Faulknerian action the grotesque resides in a simple image perceived, under stress, as symbolic, even if with a degree of surrealism. Such is the replacement of Flem's invariable cloth cap with "a hat, a new one of the broad black felt kind which country preachers and politicians wore" (*T*, 138), to mark his elevation to vice-presidency of the bank. Gavin Stevens sees the exchange in a fantastic light as he reviews "that long series of interlocked circumstances" (*T*, 140) which brought it about—Colonel Sartoris's employment of Byron Snopes as bank clerk, whose embezzling is discovered when the colonel's death in Bayard's recklessly driven car necessitates a bank audit, and De Spain's assumption of responsibility, in a dark deal (not fully explored at this point) which brings in Flem. So Gavin lets himself muse that "the single result of all this apparently was to efface that checked cap from Flem Snopes and put that hot-looking black politician-preacher's hat on him in its stead" (*T*, 140–41). Reduction can be as expressive of the grotesque as exaggeration, and by fancying the matter in such an oversimplification Gavin is coming as close as such a rational man can allow himself to an escape into incredulity from the gross effects of brutal causes, the harsh facts and cold indisputable logic of Flem Snopes's rise. It is quite the opposite from Norman Douglas's witty demonstration at the end of Chapter XXIX in *South Wind* of how a mosquito bite can cure a volcanic eruption; there superstition attributes cause and effect to sheer coincidence, and separate personal, political, and ecclesiastical interests merely happen to fall in with one another; in *The Town* Flem's progress is by calculated exploitation of every one and every thing, synthesizing to a single private end the known purposes of others and the accidents befalling them, from Eula's pregnancy to Colonel Sartoris's heart failure. So to suggest ironically that what has occurred is no more than the replacement of a cap with more formal headgear is to adumbrate the symbol of a self-hatting, an elevation that climaxes a whole history of Snopesism on the make, in a community all too vulnerable. Once more an extreme, this time minute rather than monstrous, has implied a mean. Here the grotesque in miniature is so obviously a minor detail that a glance at the totality is demanded. Through the small end of the telescope Flem's new hat may become the single conspicuous object; conversely the large view is enforced by the irony of Gavin Stevens' almost averted glance, with its implied recognition of the hat as not a badge of increased respectability but of consummated outrage. Such grotesque fancifulness as Gavin's, while it is tinged with the comic, is not for relief in the sense of escape, or a complete turning of the coin to conceal the opposite side; it is rather for relief by detachment, not a complete disengagement but an aloofness for breathing space and a perspective in which some pertinent essence of the actual is brought out.

Some of Faulkner's most striking grotesques (again, like Conrad's and like Dickens's in simpler degree) are minor characters, whom he takes time to sketch in detail and show in motion, though they may play only a brief and incidental part. There is old Het in the mule-in-the-yard episode in *The Town;* as Charles tells it, having got it from Ratliff, she just happened to be at Mrs. Hait's when I. O. Snopes's mule or one of its pursuers knocked the coal scuttle full of live ashes into the cellarway and the house burned down. First Faulkner lets Charles appreciatively recreate the local consciousness of old Het—her sleeping quarters the poor house, her fief the community, through which she passes on regular rounds with her shopping bag—

tall, lean, of a dark chocolate color, voluble, cheerful, in tennis shoes and the long rat-colored coat trimmed with what forty or fifty years ago had been fur, and the purple toque that old Mrs Compson had given her fifty years ago while General Compson himself was still alive, set on the exact top of her head rag (*T*, 231).

Unless the women lock their doors against old Het, they will find her

settled in a chair in the kitchen, having established already upon the begging visitation a tone blandly and incorrigibly social.
 She passed that way from house to house, travelling in a kind of moving island of alarm and consternation as she levied her weekly toll of food scraps and cast-off garments and an occasional coin for snuff, moving in an urbane uproar and as inescapable as a tax-gatherer (*T*, 232).

So completely self-possessed in her grotesqueness, the imperturbable and spirited old Het is happily alert to life's surrounding oddities, and can be the perfect chorus to the comic goings-on she witnessed at Mrs. Hait's; it is in her picturesque terms that the incident has passed into local lore and is recalled by Charles Mallison.
 While he does this with particular gusto, it is also with broad relevance to Snopesism, for in the figure of I. O. Snopes the grotesque is both comic and seriously thematic—indeed, as Ratliff puts it later, "soon as you set down to laugh at it, you find out it aint funny a-tall" (*T*, 257). The more sober motif proceeds from Flem; with his consciousness of blood relationship working only in reverse, he pays off I. O. Snopes to get him out of town, as another step in Flem's pursuit of respectability. In itself, however, I. O. Snopes's involvement with mules, like his earlier blacksmithing and schoolmaster-

ing, is as purely grotesque as anything in the trilogy, and can be comfortably laughed at because the indefatigable fellow is also so often ineffectual in his petty schemings. Only for one or two instants does that ineffectuality take on any pathos, and more especially for Faulkner's most sensitive spectator. On the night after the catastrophe, baffled to speechlessness, I. O. Snopes stands by the cooking fire in Mrs. Hait's back yard "with his hands to the blaze," and, as Charles reports it, "Uncle Gavin said he did look cold, small, forlorn somehow since he was so calm, so quiet" (*T*, 255). But that is an almost unparalleled pause in the man's nervously opportunistic life.

While Flem is most laconic, I. O. is the most talkative of the Snopeses. He is given to spouting portmanteau proverbs, as that "a stitch in times saves nine lives for even a cat," or that "when you dines in Rome you durn sho better watch your overcoat." Listening to him, according to Ratliff, "you stayed so busy trying to unravel just which of two or three proverbs he had jumbled together that you couldn't even tell just exactly what lie he had told you until it was already too late" (*T*, 242). Sardonically Ratliff sees some fitness, however, in this fellow's "teaching the school," in that there he had "found the one and only place in the world or Frenchman's Bend either where he not only can use them proverbs of hisn all day long but he will be paid for doing it" (*H*, 80). After I. O. had "lit out" (*H*, 303) when his deserted wife and child appeared in the hamlet, Ratliff had caricatured him as "that quick-fatherer, the Moses with his mouth full of mottoes and his coat-tail full of them already halfgrown retroactive sons" (*H*, 368). The man's incompetence as livestock dealer becomes wryly grotesque too, and not without a touch of the pathetic, as Charles reconstructs into a typical vignette I. O.'s transits across the peaceful and somnolent Jefferson scene in dust and uproar, his approach heralded by forlorn shouts and cries, his passing marked by a yellow cloud of dust filled with the tossing jug-shaped heads and the clattering hooves, then last of all Snopes himself at a panting trot, his face gaped with forlorn shouting and wrung with concern and terror and dismay (*T*, 236).

But for the pure grotesque in I. O. Snopes's adventures, nothing surpasses the primitive art of old Het's viewing, for instance when his mule in Mrs. Hait's yard happens to "coincide with a rooster and eight white-leghorn hens" and as old Het told it, according to Charles,

it looked just like something out of the Bible, or maybe out of some kind of hoodoo witches' Bible: the mule that came out of the fog to begin with like a hant or a goblin, now kind of soaring back into the fog again borne on a cloud of little winged ones (*T*, 238).

Old Het is but one of Faulkner's troupe of commoners who demonstrate fanciful vision as a natural function, along with a spontaneous folk expressiveness extending to the grotesque, whether comic or melancholy-ironic.

The extravagant-grotesque at its most conspicuous is only one facet of Faulkner's own characteristically opulent mode. He is adept with focused episode, rapid dialogue, and the epitomizing image, but pointed though he can be, he is never a spare writer, and his conceivings as well as imaginings are explosively compact of imagination. His fullness and recurrent flamboyance, often criticized, can scarcely be judged aright, however, unless this is seen voicing his responsiveness to the complexities of his characters, their situations, and his fictional themes. Not all the elaborateness of expression proceeds from intensely self-conscious and perturbed characters, such as Gavin Stevens or Hightower or Quentin Compson, or from the more provincial and less sophisticated, whether a

Ratliff or an old Het; sometimes it is Faulkner himself, in what may seem a virtuoso's inserted cadenza unless it is read in largest dramatic and thematic context. Thus the description of summer rain in *The Hamlet*:

The pine-snoring wind dropped, then gathered; in an anticlimax of complete vacuum the shaggy pelt of earth became overblown like that of a receptive mare for the rampant crash, the furious brief fecundation which, still rampant, seeded itself in flash and glare of noise and fury and then was gone, vanished; then the actual rain, from a sky already breaking as if of its own rich over-fertile weight, running in a wild lateral turmoil among the unrecovered leaves, not in drops but in needles of fiery ice which seemed to be not trying to fall but, immune to gravity, earthless, were merely trying to keep pace with the windy uproar which had begotten and foaled them, striking in thin brittle strokes through his hair and shirt and against his lifted face, each brief lance already filled with the glittering promise of its imminent cessation like the brief bright saltless tears of a young girl over a lost flower; then gone too, fled north and eastward beyond the chromatic arch of its own insubstantial armistice, leaving behind it the spent confetti of its carnival to gather and drip leaf by leaf and twig by twig then blade by blade of grass, to gather in murmuring runnels, releasing in mirrored repetition the sky which, glint by glint of fallen gold and blue, the falling drops had prisoned (*H*, 211).

This must be estimated, of course, for its function as counter-point and contrasting backdrop to the idiot Ike Snopes's infatuated carrying off of the cow; typically Faulkner is using the discrepant for an irony which can allow a pathos even to the sordid. In passing it should be noted too that this prose, so richly detailed, is not in the least verbose; it is instead poetic, in that true sense which is the very opposite of the diffuse or the prolix—the concentratedly apt, the quickly implicative, as in this rain "running in a wild lateral turmoil among the unrecovered leaves."

Faulkner's awareness of complexity, when delegated to his spectator-characters, not only produces their typical procedure of sustained speculation, with their minds as mirrors not fixed but turned to tentative angles; it also pauses to pin down as best may be with whole series of words some single glimpse of the faceted moment. The consequent opulence takes on a quality of the baroque, its drift as accented statement toward the grotesque. Thus Quentin Compson, in *Absalom, Absalom!,* listening to Miss Rosa Coldfield's story, sits through "the long still hot weary dead September afternoon" near a window where wistaria (like the events recalled) is "blooming for the second time," while into it "sparrows came now and then in random gusts, making a dry vivid dusty sound" and Miss Coldfield talks on "in that grim haggard amazed voice" until "the long-dead object of her impotent yet indomitable frustration," Sutpen, "would appear, as though by outraged recapitulation evoked, quiet inattentive and harmless, out of the biding and dreamy and victorious dust" (*AA*, 7, 8). This represents a very complex realization and a resultant intensity of mood, but it is subjective and descriptive rather than expressed and definitive as in Hamlet's rage against a "Bloody, bawdy villain!" or his realistic elegy for a "wretched, rash, intruding fool." The extraordinary phraseology of that first paragraph in *Absalom, Absalom!* or in such picturings as of the summer storm in *The Hamlet* may be ruled out by the kind of classicist who insists that all prose should be prosaic, but a more liberal view may allow the fictionist something of the imaginative language traditional in drama and may even feel that such lyric effects as in Arnold's superbly cumulative line, "The unplumbed, salt, estranging sea," can be emulated in narrative art without impropriety.

At a lesser level, such verse as Whitman's categorizing or

the Reverend Gilbert White's nice title, "On the Dark, Still, Dry, Warm Weather," may suggest some similar legitimacy in Charles Mallison's report that "Mr de Spain's bank continued its ordinary sober busy prosperous gold-auraed course" (*T*, 309). It is only with "gold-auraed" that Charles goes beyond the scrupulously definitive level of White's phrase, but it is not into vagueness, and in adding something connotative it is not verbose, for the prolonged paces of the adjectives suggest an uninterrupted, as the words themselves suggest a mundane, procedure. Faulkner's full phraseology can have a more urgent movement about it too; Tom Tom, the Negro fireman at the power plant, is a real dramatic figure when, as Charles imagines it from Gowan's telling, "presently there he was, with his little high hard round intractable cannon-ball head" (*T*, 28), and this is just right and no more than Tom Tom's due, for he is of the rare ones who have bested Flem Snopes.

Faulkner himself and some of his chosen characters in the trilogy, in moving from close scrutiny to wide speculation, will sort out alternatives, rejecting one in favor of another, with definition given a varied antiphonal setting, creating the quest for truth and for its furthest refinement as a real part of the narrative momentum. Thus Tull is seen in *The Hamlet*, weeks after the accident with the spotted horse, cleanly on Saturday in washed and ironed overalls:

the sedate and innocent blue of his eyes above the month-old corn-silk beard which concealed most of his abraded face and which gave him an air of incredible and paradoxical dissoluteness, not as though at last and without warning he had appeared in the sight of his fellowmen in his true character, but as if an old Italian portrait of a child saint had been defaced by a vicious and idle boy (*H*, 369).

At other times alternatives are allowed to stand, hedging in the reality, however fantastically, as concerning Flem's "tiny predatory nose like the beak of a small hawk," seen

as though the original nose had been left off by the original designer or craftsman and the unfinished job taken over by someone of a radically different school or perhaps by some viciously maniacal humorist or perhaps by one who had had only time to clap into the center of the face a frantic and desperate warning (*H*, 59).

It is often thus; where alternatives fade off into uncertainty, complexity becomes enigmatic, and this Faulkner himself and his characters repeatedly face, and the grotesque becomes the acknowledgment of reality. A plain and characteristic example is at the very conclusion of *The Town,* when Charles, describing the departure of the four half-breed children Flem was sending back to Byron in El Paso by day coach (its steps "like a narrow dropped jaw") says he and Ratliff "watched them mount and vanish one by one into that iron impatient maw," and last of all the "least un in its ankle-length single garment like a man's discarded shirt made out of flour- or meal-sacking or perhaps the remnant of an old tent. We never did know which it was" (*T*, 371). As a close to a many-peopled, elaborately-plotted novel, that seven-word sentence might be called trivial, but it will scarcely seem so to careful readers. Faulkner is sometimes elaborate, sometimes pointed, sometimes subtle, sometimes emphatic, but he is never trivial. Furthermore, he never throws away a curtain line; every work of his has as careful a resolution, thematically and aesthetically, as a sound fine musical composition. Thus is it at the conclusion of *Sanctuary,* with the equivocal Temple and her father sitting in the Luxembourg Gardens, where the band plays: "Rich and resonant the brasses crashed and died in the thick green twilight . . . where at sombre intervals the dead tranquil queens in stained marble mused. . . ." Quite differently, but quite as much to its own point, *Absalom, Absalom!* closes with Quentin's meeting Shreve's question, "Why do you hate the South?" by a quick answer, twice over, and then reiterated in his thoughts, with too much protestation: *"I dont. I dont! I dont hate it! I dont hate it!"* All along in *The Town* questions have reverberated, set going not only by natural curiosity but by the humane concern of Gavin, Ratliff, and Charles, whose inquiries are Faulkner's medium throughout this novel, as they are to be in part in *The Mansion,* where even in its finalities there is still so much about which, as about that least un's shirt, it can only be said that "we never did know." So in all Faulkner's full style, with its epithets, its alternative speculations, its multifariously detailed imagery, and its juxtaposition of the sharply factual and the fantastic, there is nevertheless the opposite of any pretense to complete comprehension and definitiveness, but rather the hint, by extensions that fade out like searchlights into space, as to the only partially penetrable mysteries of being and conduct. And this can be implied by the grotesque as it goes beyond exaggeration, even to distortion, in a mirage-like view declaring its authenticity through an ardent atmosphere's shimmering refractions, and in a voice thrown back across a wildness as a changed unmistakable echo.

Linda becomes a chief case in point. Widowed and deafened in Spain in the ideologically most crucial of modern wars, with her quacking voice and the tablet for Gavin to write on, living with Flem her not-father in his ill-gotten mansion, in a suspension of her womanly life that makes her seem a lady bewitched in an ogre's castle, where she herself turns avenger, she is certainly a figure shadowed and weird. Yet she has a basic reality, in her own fate and as to its sources. She is companion to other quite different Faulkner figures, all portrayed with similarly extreme strokes—to the poor-white, abused, laconically enduring Mrs. Armstid of *The Hamlet;* to Joanna Burden of *Light in August,* the racked victim of history, heredity, repression, and chance; and to Eula, Linda's mother, bartered to Flem in *The Hamlet* and caught, in *The Town,* between an illicit passion and maternal love and driven to suicide. Strangeness in these women is the scar inflicted by external evil; similarly Linda, for all her grotesqueness, is universalized as victim. It is a tortuous path she follows from a Greenwich Village love affair through injurious war to soiling manual labor in another war's shipyard and a return to loneliness in her nominal home, but in all this she is so vulnerable a woman as to make basic the indictment against circumstance which is typically afflictive, however grotesque in detail.

Not incompatible with pathos, the grotesque in any such characters may even serve to rhetorize the tragic, especially through acute intense tropes. So it is as Eula sat in Stevens' office and he notes her "cigarette burning on the tray, balancing its muted narrow windless feather," while her face is seen looking

out of the half-shadow above the rim of light from the lamp—the big broad simple still unpainted beautiful mouth, the eyes not the hard and dusty blue of fall but the blue of spring blooms, all one inextricable mixture of wistaria cornflowers larkspur bluebells weeds and all, all the lost girls' weather and boys' luck and too late the grief, too late the grief, too late (*T,* 332).

So too the extremes that bound the rising-falling action of Linda's story are marked by unusual figures of immunity and inviolability; Gavin verifies Charles's vision of her in her girlhood as like "the young pointer bitch . . . immune now in virginity . . . not proud and not really oblivious: just immune in intensity and ignorance and innocence as the sleepwalker is for the moment immune from the anguishes and agonies of breath" (*T*, 132), and then Charles himself sees the returned war-deafened widow as "the inviolate bride of silence" (*M*, 203), "absolved of mundanity . . . . forever inviolate and private in solitude" (*M*, 211), "the bride of silence more immaculate in that chastity than ever Caesar's wife because she was invulnerable too, forever safe" (*M*, 216). The shading of the grotesque into the pathetic is repeatedly pointed to by a single word; Gavin, in his last interview with Eula, had called young Linda "lost" (*T*, 330), whether (as he presumed) Eula were to take her away with herself and Manfred or whether she were left behind; Charles over and over calls the deafened Linda "lost" (*M*, 219, 222). Then when Gavin and Linda grow abstract over the untimely deaths of promising artists such as Kohl, and Linda has asked what poetry could "match giving your life to say No to people like Hitler and Mussolini," and Gavin, declaring her "absolutely right," has added that "Nothing is ever lost," Charles thinks, "Except Linda of course" (*M*, 218). In terms of the Faulknerian theme any remembrance of the heroic is greatly and enduringly effective, so that Gavin is right; but Charles is right too, Linda is lost, widowed and immured disabled in solitariness. Thereby her grotesqueness, merging into the pathetic, deepens to the tragic; character stands forth to validate plot at the conceptual level, as idiosyncrasy keeps vivified in the representative situation the unique human sufferer. The grotesque simile of the pointer bitch to figure a dainty adolescent innocence still immune makes way for the actual grotesque of the deafened widowed woman with the quacking voice and the writing tablet, for whom the rest is a silence that is her last defense, an inviolable one because also an isolation not only from sound but from any quick ready sharing, whether in ordinary talk or, as Charles imagines it, in the murmuring and close whispering when there is "more of love and excitement and ecstasy than just one can bear" (*M*, 217).

Grotesqueness of appearance or act in such a fictional figure, passing beyond sensationalism or mere picturesqueness, may mark a serious art, and be its peculiarly effective means. The aberrations which victims of conflict are driven to may become indexes in reverse of values soliciting affirmation; when the beholder is led to protest that "it shouldn't happen, shouldn't be" (cf. *M*, 79), the eccentric and even the outrageous, however extreme its arc, is seen turning upon a center of judgment. And in such evocative employment of the grotesque, the artist goes far beyond not only the contraptions of popular stories but certain implications of social science often absorbed into more pretentious fiction, where the abnormal has been employed at an extreme opposite to the humanistic artist's uses. For the statistician the abnormal is defined simply by its degree of variance from a median in objective data. For the humanist the norm is a tentative stage on an aspiring uncertain passage in being and becoming, a foothold known as precarious and valued relatively, for what further access to remote goals it allows. In the narrative arts, whether fiction or drama, such a view—and it is Faulkner's— by seeing reality pregnant with values liable to distortion or negation, excludes both a fatalistic determinism and the sentimentality or slam-bang of melodrama, as set forth in the black and white of absolute evil (eradicable by good shooting) and absolute good (attainable as connubial bliss in a disaster-proof cottage).

The great modern split between popular and serious fiction, and drama too, has been on these latter grounds. Platitudes, chiefly of an exculpatory or soothing sort, are parabolized as a complete orthodoxy, its crowning reward a presently attainable all's-well ever-after. In nothing is Faulkner more eminently the serious artist than in his devotion of fiction to the opposite, the tentative persistent exploration of a fluent complexity never entirely scrutable, allowing approaches to values but never promising arrival at absolute ends. Faulkner should be approved therefore, under the sort of attitude which R. P. Blackmur cites—the "consciously provisional, speculative, and dramatic" employment of concept, as is to be found in the early Plato and in Montaigne, "archetypes of unindoctrinated thinking," Plato holding "conflicting ideas in shifting balance, presenting them in contest and evolution," Montaigne "always making room for another idea, and implying always a third for provisional, adjudicating irony." While a novel's representational techniques differentiate it, of course, from philosophy or essay of even the liveliest sort, as in Plato or Montaigne, yet perhaps no more comprehensive definition of the art of fiction could be stated than one phrased in Blackmur's terms, "concept" in a "use" that is "consciously provisional, speculative, and dramatic."[6] And Blackmur's setting up such a criterion against its opposite, doctrine become dogma, provides as well a basis for rejecting the degenerate art of that voluminous storytelling which makes an hypnotic ritual of either platitude or propaganda.

Nor is the serious and speculative artist in fiction, such as Faulkner, different only from the popular purveyors of tales; he goes beyond another type, the all too sober, indubitably factual, but scarcely speculative naturalist. Since in social science the variation from the norm takes on its own statistical stability, resting on a predictable percentage of cases to be found at any particular stage of aberration, naturalistic fiction and drama will ape this bare precision, and stop at just the point where the humanistic artist, confronted by grotesqueness in a life, is moved to speculations conditioned

[6] *The Double Agent* (New York, 1935), pp. 271, 273.

by concepts of a more nearly symmetrized personality, and thereby examines action not just by statistical norms of behavior but by ideals of conduct, concerning which any approaches or deviations are colored as varieties of fortune and fate. The humanistic provisional thus energizes the dramatic in ways that the factual, however positive, could never do alone.

Seen in context, the darkly shaded grotesquerie in Faulkner's works is neither obscuration nor clap-trap, as impercipients have accused him of—sometimes in stubborn persistence, clinging to the end of a limb gone out on. Even at its most intense and extreme it is for thematic emphasis, by those main bold lines which as in caricature bound the concept at its limits and thereby starkly contain basic implication. Neither is Faulkner the calculating virtuoso of symbolism some loftier criticism alleges. In his hands the grotesque becomes means of a searching realism, corresponding vividly to the central fact that evil conduct born of obsessions distorts the natural and defeats the human potential, with the corollary that even at its best, in resisting evil, right intention can fall short, into the partial, the inadequate, or carry over into the preposterous. As grotesqueness thus enters into a resistance of the exaggerated forms which evil takes, the crusades of Faulkner's champions become a series of sallies afoot, and virtually bare-handed, so to speak, but this too is realism. Where find the complete and proper champion, this side of romantic melodrama? It takes Gavin Stevens, V. K. Ratliff, and Charles Mallison as a vigilant committee, and even so they often fumble, Gavin most of all, since although most experienced he is also made susceptible by being most personally and sensitively concerned. Yet despite their inescapable human fallibility, how can such thinking-feeling men refuse to oppose the enemies of propriety and wholesomeness and to aid the victims of such enmity? And how close the mind against inquiry aiming at the definition of principle and for that means of grace, an ideal purpose? It is in these terms of civilized man's running battle with fate and his worse fellows, as a common and continuous ordeal, that Faulkner's spectator-interventionists have their being; consequently in them too eccentricity implies a center, as in all his characters aberration becomes the negative definition of the norm, in a whole creation which groans and travails.

7

"the sloped whimsical ironic hand out of Mississippi attenuated"

A brooding over experience itself, turning around and about the event, has always been a main mode of Faulkner's art, being his mind's way and core of his temperament. It may seem to point toward a more particular question concerning extravagance. Not necessarily as to the drama itself, however, in its somber rendition; the recurrent nightmare aspect of life in Yoknapatawpha County is no more appalling than a present actuality of which many are sufficiently conscious to have bad dreams about it, and to wake to find the fact of the matter more terrifying and more baffling than the dream. If Faulkner is unduly, unrealistically extravagant, perhaps it is rather in endowing many different well-intentioned characters not only with percipience but with a flair for expressing it ironically, often with a consequent trend toward the grotesque. A reserved judgment seems called for. Just as it would take a sentimentalist wearing glasses of deepest rose

167

to deny the reality of that distorting malevolence Faulkner has depicted in many guises, so it would be a bold cynic who would assert that certain people are not as discerning and also calmly wry-voiced as Faulkner makes many of them. Exaggeration or not, in its way it is the most hopeful thing Faulkner has said about the South, or about his larger subject, humanity.

Its epitome is Ratliff, the indigenous, ubiquitous, wily, and detached, manifesting undemonstratively his humane outlook, "quizzical, maybe speculative, but not bemused" (*M*, 232). He represents most purely Faulkner's developed use of witnesses and first-person testifiers. This goes beyond the customary immediate authenticating narrative device, though that convention as such is brilliantly employed in the trilogy, and with some originality in its weaving together of separate testimonies. Beyond that, Ratliff and others are poetizers of the fable, transmuting the historical into the imaginative, enhancing it for the delineation of theme, vivifying it by sympathy, focusing upon it by the refractions of irony. This effect is conditioned by each witness's particular temperament, as it determines insight, fancy, and vein of style as may be, but all Faulkner's poetizers of the fable are professional to some degree, in that they are ironists. Faulkner's uses of fictional technique to get his story set down are admirable in themselves, but the real sweep and grace of these gestures is in how he lets it be sensed, and its greatest consequent power is in its subtle command of recollection and reflection in the mode of an inclusive empathy and humane judiciousness. The modest Ratliff, steady, sensible, and calm, contributes greatly to this effect by giving its sources a norm. He stands at the center of a scale, with Mink Snopes at one end in his sharp sarcastic retorts to Houston, and at the other extreme Gavin Stevens, with his informed intelligence, his gallant

disinterestedness, and his acute, sometimes anguished concern, comprehending everything from the materialistic flab-
biness of American democracy to the pathos of adolescent
girls flowering in a town and a world that will not sufficiently
cherish them—and with Gavin himself summing up an aspect
of modernity, in that the rational and impulsive are so mixed
in him as to provoke his irony at the expense of his own un-
rest. Charles too has mastered the idiom of this outlook and
mood, though he speaks it with his own accent. So do minor
characters, such as the Warden at Parchman. Such irony
manifests a competence to deal with the multiple and the
incongruous, and not to be utterly confused by it, much less
disconcerted, and this peculiar wryness suggests an aplomb
that without detracting from dramatic urgency keeps perspectives wide.

Yet the actors' irony, even as a serviceable artifice and a
pervasive tone making for aesthetic unity, is not all. The
voices have their master, and they exist within his personal
vision of the human condition, in an evoked climate more
than county-wide. Faulkner's creative dominance has been
hitherto disapproved by some, but this perhaps comes of
giving too much weight to certain restrictive conventions in
current fiction. A larger view discerns how in the arts magnitude always casts its recognizable shadow, how unmistakable is the thumbprint, the slant of the script—Faulkner's, like
Mr. Compson's, "sloped whimsical ironic hand out of Mississippi attenuated" (*AA*, 377)—and how mystically omnipresent a potent artist is in any world and work of his own
making. Hitherto the idiosyncratic stamp of temperament
upon major creations has not only been noted but valued,
sui generis—in Milton or Hopkins, Rembrandt or Matisse,
Beethoven or Delius, Shakespeare or Molière, Jane Austen
or Thomas Mann. Every name evokes a style, but behind

style a choice of matter, and behind that an imperiously originative personality. Since the fictionist or dramatist bequeaths to the deserving children of his mind his most precious holdings, his tastes and attitudes and even the images of their formulation, it is not surprising if Faulkner is detectable in Mink's perception of Old Ike McCaslin's integrity: "He has done spent too much time in the woods with deer and bears and panthers that either are or they aint, right quick and now and not no shades between. He wont know how to believe a lie even if I could tell him one" (*M*, 31). It is as plainly Faulkner behind Gavin's diatribe in the thirties:

"That one already in Italy and one a damned sight more dangerous in Germany because all Mussolini has to work with are Italians while this other man has Germans. And the one in Spain that all he needs is to be let alone a little longer by the rest of us who still believe that if we just keep our eyes closed long enough it will all go away" (*M*, 160).

This too will be allowed as fiction by anyone who has not closed his eyes and hoped apprehensive men like Gavin Stevens would go away; there indeed are those who are more acutely conscious of our terrifying one world than of the local weather, and the dramatization of their personal concern, the vocalization of their human anguish, is a function of realistic art.

More importantly, though, and beyond such occasional emergence of abstractions, Faulkner's creation is permeated by the spirit in which he has seized upon his concepts, a concern so ardent that it impregnates the whole work aesthetically and exists as an emanation from it. Each of the four sections in *The Hamlet*, like movements in a symphony, has its key and tempo and particular mood, and within each its counterpointing and modulations. In *The Mansion* such a predominating atmosphere, generated by the rare force of Faulkner's imagination, and extending to the grotesque, is to be chiefly felt as of the two disparate and differently realized figures, Linda and Mink. Linda is seen from three main angles, through Gavin, Ratliff, and Charles, and also in refractions produced by their views of each others' views, sometimes in dialogue, sometimes in their subjectively centered first-person recapitulations, both often ironic. The resultant picture of her, a genuine grotesque, is a faceted, almost fractured representation, like a Picasso multiple-profile face. Just as in Picasso there is a transcendence of the restriction to any one view, so in Faulkner's study of Linda by three interlocutors there is no diminishing reduction to an isolated aspect; rather she appears instantly in all the contiguous mortal dimensions of time and her total conditionings by heredity and by past and present circumstances. It is a remarkable execution so to have suspended the sense of a whole life of one who could be said scarcely to have had a moment to herself apart from her role as victim. That what repeatedly victimizes Linda is aggression, whether in personal, social, or ideological terms, makes her a main figure in Faulkner's development of theme from *The Town* on to the trilogy's end. That she is preserved for the reader less by her own assertions (drastic as some of them are) than through the individualized views of a trio of commentators (one of them also a devoted aide) makes *The Town* and *The Mansion* a further expression of Faulkner's own moral conviction, through his faith in its presence in personalities as various as Gavin, Ratliff, and Charles. That the grotesque, intensified by severally overlaid views of it, is made to enhance the essence of an authentic and representative subject of realistic fiction is a particular aesthetic triumph. That the presentation of Linda in *The Mansion* is quite different from that of Mink, as both differ from the setting-forth of Flem, shows not only Faulkner's technical command but his faithfulness to the variety of persons and events themselves, multiplied almost infinitely by the ways they impinge and thus complicate situations and experience.

This complex reality is not abstracted or attenuated; it is dramatized in sharply illuminative scenes, rapidly successive or prolonged at a sustained pace, but always pointed. Faulkner's fiction, like most great narrative and dramatic works, turns upon epiphanal moments, when crucial realization is precipitated out of the circumstantial flux. This may be an objective manifestation to the reader, as when Flem at the conclusion of *The Hamlet,* having glanced at his latest victim, the deceived and besotted Armstid digging for buried money at Frenchman's Bend, "spat over the wagon wheel" and "jerked the reins slightly," on his way to Jefferson out of the rural community he had thoroughly exploited. The epiphany may be subjective, an inclusive vision like Hightower's reverie in "the final copper light of afternoon" (*LA,* 441). Scarcely anywhere, however, has Faulkner represented a character's more complicated and poignant experience than in Gavin Stevens' farewell view of Linda and his connections with her, and never has Faulkner offered the reader a revelation with a more reticent yet richly implicative art, or a more subtle transmuting of the grotesque into the pathetic.

Gavin had not only defended young Linda's faith as well as he could, he had sought to preserve certain illusions of his own about her. As a man both worldly-wise and aware of faults in his own society, he is not shaken by her uncertified alliance with Kohl or her passing involvement with Communist politics, seeing all this as a youthful quest for the dream (*M,* 151, 157), and seeking only to protect Linda from local animosities. So when Linda asks that Mink's release be advanced two years by a pardon, Gavin tries to think of her as merely merciful, and coöperates to promote the understanding that Mink is to have his freedom and a quarterly remittance if he will leave Mississippi at once and stay away (*M*, 369, 374). While the pardon is being arranged and later after Mink, released, has disappeared, the skeptical Ratliff plagues Gavin with the faintest ironic hints (*M*, 368, 372, 377) that Linda knows what Mink will do. Then after Mink has shot Flem (and as the reader has seen, Linda has handed him the pistol he dropped and has directed him to the door for escape) Gavin discovers that Linda's order for the foreign car she leaves Jefferson in had been placed as soon as Mink's pardon was assured (*M*, 423). Thus when Ratliff suggests Linda brought about Mink's release to avoid her mother's reproaches in heaven for not having seen vengeance done upon Flem, Gavin can say nothing, and his tears are indicated only by Ratliff's handing him a clean handkerchief (*M*, 431), whereas earlier after Eula's burial, tears had run down his face unwiped, with the drink Ratliff had mixed for him sitting untasted on his desk (*T*, 359; *M*, 150).

The nature of Gavin's latest grief, undefined, is to be sensed from its sources in the trilogy. His is no mere conventional regret or shock that the cherished Linda has been accessory before the fact of a murder and has similarly involved him. It seems rather a lament for all that Linda has been through, and he with her, the loss and grief and ghastly wrongs endured with that fortitude which is also a numbing, perhaps a hardening, and above all a distortion. What Linda is driven to mirrors what it has been like for her to have been so driven. Thus the grotesque becomes the pathetic; irony in its very detachment is the more comprehending; the absurd is lifted to the level of the tragic by humane regret. *Sunt lacrimae rerum*—except as such Gavin Stevens' undescribed tears are indescribable, and as such they resemble those which Byron Bunch sees run like sweat down the cheeks of Hightower (*LA*, 344) when he was burdened with the woes of Joe Christmas and his grandmother; Gavin's are like Dilsey's tears in the Negro church on Easter morning, sliding "down her fallen cheeks, in and out of the myriad coruscations of immolation and abnegation and time" (*SF*, 368), and continuing unchecked as she walked back to her endless labors for the decadent Compsons she chided and pampered; Gavin's tears are like those the retired French Quartermaster General, at the conclusion of *A Fable*, shed over the bloodied but invincible English veteran, also a devotee.

Thus throughout Faulkner's works it is to be seen that the ultimate ironies are life's, and they are not little. The grotesque becomes relevant medium of a broadly realistic fiction as it traces the tangents and extents of folly, malefaction, and distracting grief. Central to such an art is a pressing humane concern, often projected dramatically as judgment and intervention, and constantly sensed as the validating mode, creating, as Conrad says, "the moral, the emotional atmosphere." With feeling and conviction as the begetters of action, action itself becomes considerable as conduct, and while discrepancy may elicit tears, these really assert the unsurrendered though relatively inaccessible ideal, by that margin of the positive which separates tragedy from despair.

It is concerning Mink, however, that the Faulknerian tone emerges most familiarly, meticulously realistic and boldly intense, and with the resonance of a sustained solicitude. All the chapters centered on Mink's struggle with Houston and Flem and impersonal obstacle are conveyed within the limitations of that wretched obsessed little man's consciousness, yet made striking by his pathetically morbid purpose and by the grotesque shadowing-forth of his animal endurance, stealth, and relentlessness. In no comparable character—not even Joe Christmas—has Faulkner rounded out a more living composite of diverse traits than in Mink, whose aspect a deepening pathos does not soften. He is "waiflike and abandoned . . . but no more pitiable than a scorpion" (*M*, 287), while his vindictiveness wears an aura of honor, dimly but in archetype, through a facing up to both adversary and adversity, with endurance as life's irreducible integer, the last resource for a brave brutal quest persisted in against terrific odds. This is touched upon in *The Hamlet* and more closely traced in several passages in *The Mansion*, as the released Mink hitchhikes from Parchman to Memphis to buy a gun. He finds himself not just old—he has reached his grand climacteric—but also an obsolescent man, after thirty-eight years of imprisonment. He "had forgotten distance" (259), cars and trucks not wagons now rush along highways hard-paved (103, 104), and he puzzles over the "new iron numbers along the roads," so different from "the hand-lettered mile boards" he remembered (403). Tinned sardines which were five cents are now twenty-six (259), and he thinks, "If bread could jump up ten cents right while I was looking at it, maybe I can't buy a pistol even for the whole thirteen dollars" (263)—which was all he had before he bought food and allowed himself the wild indulgence of two coca-colas (260).

The world Mink reënters bewilders him not only by its strangeness but by inconsistencies. It is largely inimical, yet he encounters some good will. Though a country storekeeper cheats him (261) and the migrant worker at evangelist Goodyhay's place steals Mink's money (273), a man in Goodyhay's little congregation makes that up for him (282), and the Negro for whom he picks cotton not only serves Mink supper first and alone but says, "I don't charge nobody to eat at my

house" (400)—a complementary instance of propriety maintained in low estate. The antitheses continue; one Memphis
policeman, finding Mink on a park bench at night, gives him
fifty cents to get a bed; Mink thinks this part of "the new
laws . . . he had heard about . . . in Parchman . . . Relief or
W P and A" (287), and so at the depot when another policeman jerks him awake and tells him to get out, Mink waits for
"the half a dollar" and must dodge the man's irritation (289).
Old, ignorant, weary, yet intent, Mink continues, telling himself, "A man can get through anything if he can jest keep on
walking" (289).

Below such a plain surface as this—Mink's minimal verbal-
izing of his plight and purpose—lies a tension controlled this
side desperation only by his indomitable will. The submerged
emotion is always felt, however, and one means of its con-
veyance is in the sense of setting, suggested as to its impact
upon this poor little old man bent on murder. Faulkner has
given the nightmare of Mink's impeded obsessive progress
through space and circumstance an almost surrealistic expression, as in the hitchhiker's approach to Memphis

at night, the dark earth on either hand and ahead already random and spangled with the neon he had never seen before, and
in the distance the low portentous glare of the city itself, he sitting on the edge of the seat as a child sits, almost as small as a
child, peering ahead as the car rushed, merging into one mutual
spangled race bearing toward, as though by the acceleration of
gravity or suction, the distant city . . . as if all the earth was
hurrying, plunging, being sucked, decked with diamond and
ruby lights, into the low glare on the sky . . . (*M*, 283).

The tone is maintained as the rootless, all but resourceless
man wanders the city late at night, and coming away from
the chill of "the River . . . the vast and vacant expanse, only
the wet dark cold blowing" (286), approaches a down-town
square, where he finds

the glare and the murmur, the resonant concrete hum, though unsleeping still, now had a spent quality like rising fading smoke or steam, so that what remained of it was now high among the ledges and cornices; the random automobiles which passed now, though gleaming with colored lights still, seemed now as though fleeing in terror, in solitude from solitude (*M*, 287).

However, the world reëntered has not proved altogether strange and fantastic for Mink. In the first surge of sensed release as he began his hitchhike from Parchman to Memphis, he rediscovered the seasons, and it being "almost October," he remembers an autumn day in his childhood, a golden hickory tree, and a whole incident which becomes an epiphany in nostalgia. The recollection is of his stepmother, ill from a beating by his father, asking the child to shoot a squirrel, needing "to relish something else" than "the fatback, the coarse meal, the molasses which as far as he knew was the only food all people ate except when they could catch or kill something" (*M*, 105). Lugging the shotgun taller than himself, risking a severe beating if his father found out, and staking the errand itself on the one shell he had, he tremblingly took the squirrel back to "the gaunt harried slattern of a woman" on whom he could "depend," not for help, for she was helpless too, "but for constancy, to be always there and always aware of him" (*M*, 105). Now after over half a century the tree itself would be gone, he imagines, but the memory of it remains, "golden and splendid with October," and he realizes

it aint a place a man wants to go back to; the place dont even need to be there no more. What aches a man to go back to is what he remembers (*M*, 106).

Real, deep-rooted, and human as that ache is, it is put aside, just as apparently he had ceased to speculate about his wife and daughters, and he is seen on the sunlit Memphis street, eating his frugal breakfast of animal crackers, and wrapped in the vengeful purpose which comes before all other thought of the past, as he unknowingly goes by the whorehouse where "his younger daughter was now the madam" (*M*, 290). His is the paradoxical stability of obsession, he is mild and even conciliatory in everything except his main intention, and moving about Memphis "frail and harmless and not much larger than a child" (*M*, 104), he seems almost childlike in his singleness of mind, except for its fierceness and persistence. He has kept his head and held as well to his principles; not only does this hot-tempered man remain cool, this murderer bent on another murder has reminded the storekeeper of the two coca-colas—for which Mink was then overcharged (*M*, 261), and although a gun is the one thing he must have, he would not steal Goodyhay's (*M*, 274).

After his weary nightwatch in Memphis Mink got a rusty pistol at a pawnshop and stealthily made his way into Jefferson at dusk. Still it was not easy. He managed to slip in to the mansion while the sheriff's posted guard was off duty, and he found Flem with feet propped against the mantel, but when Mink pulled the trigger there was only "the dull foolish almost inattentive click" (*M*, 415), just as years before when he ambushed Houston the first shotgun shell had failed, "the vain click louder than thunderbolt" (*H*, 250). Again it is only by sensory distortion that the intensity of Mink's experience is conveyed—in *The Hamlet* the explosion of the second shell was "the crash which after the other deafening click he did not hear at all" (250), and in *The Mansion,* after Mink with "grimed shaking child-sized hands like the hands of a pet coon" has had to "roll the cylinder back one notch so that the shell would come again under the hammer" (415), when it fires and Flem's "curious half-stifled convulsive surge" carries him over in his chair, "it seemed to him, Mink, that the report of the pistol was nothing but that when the chair finished falling and crashed to the floor, the sound would wake all Jefferson" (416).

Then the presence Mink has sensed in the house manifests itself; Linda appears and hands him back the empty pistol he has reflexively thrown at her and shows him the way out (416). With his long-meditated revenge achieved, and at the entrance of a now revealed accomplice whose gesture of returning his weapon is a kind of absolution, Mink ceases to be the man of violence, grotesque in his obsession, and his further progress becomes quiet epilogue to a life that had been almost constantly beset and embittered. Having seen him through that with increasingly vivid and empathetic narration, Faulkner carries him beyond it and into higher levels, especially in those passages toward the end where Mink becomes archetypal in his awareness of the pull of the ground on a man, "to draw you back down into it," that "power and drag of the earth" against which womenfolk must support the infant, "the old patient biding unhurried" earth which even the strong man napping upon it wakes to find "has already taken that first light holt" on him (*M*, 402, 403). This knowledge in Mink as an old man, after he has murdered Flem and has escaped westward, lets him feel community at last, knowing his individual life will "creep, seep, flow easy as sleeping . . . down and down into the ground already full of the folks that had the trouble but were free now" (*M*, 435) —there (in a Faulknerian echo), beneath what the hamlet's idiot Snopes had trodden over unknowing, "the woven canopy of blind annealing grass-roots and the roots of trees, dark in the blind dark of time's silt and rich refuse—the constant and unslumbering anonymous worm-glut and the inextricable known bones" (*H*, 207)—and Mink to be "himself among them, equal to any, good as any, brave as any, being inextricable from, anonymous with all of them" (*M*, 435).

With those polysyllables the narration has transcended Mink's powers, and now the style rises in a characterization, like a great crowded Renaissance painting, of "all of them" as "the beautiful, the splendid, the proud and the brave, right on up to the very top itself among the shining phantoms and dreams which are the milestones of the long human record-ing—Helen and the bishops, the kings and the unhomed angels, the scornful and graceless seraphim" (*M*, 435–36). Those last two adjectives (an imaging not unlike Fra Lippo Lippi's winged urchins), with their enlarging touch of the grotesque, bring Faulkner's whole subject into view, appre-hending the ineffable within the bounds of human imagina-tion. The seraphim, that highest order of angels, fervent in love, six-winged but with human hands and feet, have re-peatedly descended into the world of the trilogy, seeming the symbols of an ironic dualism pertaining to certain human beings, creatures not a little lower but of equal station with an angel fallen, fearful and wonderful. In *The Town* Gavin speculates that Flem may seek revenge on Eula's lover, Man-fred de Spain, considered as the community's "arch-fiend among sinners," the "supremely damned among the lost in-fernal seraphim" (270). In *The Mansion* Ratliff has seen Gavin, passing beyond his concern for the irredeemable Eula to an anxiety about Linda's future, as "unenchanted now . . . done freed at last of that fallen seraphim" (135). Much earlier, the allusion has occurred in *The Hamlet* in a wider and stranger context, the lyricized episode of Ike Snopes and the cow, first picturing "the slowing neap of noon, the flood, the slack of peak and crown of light garlanding all within one single coronet the fallen and unregenerate seraphim" un-named (210). Then three pages further in *The Hamlet* the passage which is to close *The Mansion* is foreshadowed almost completely, as in late afternoon the idiot comes back to the object of his passion:

Blond too in that gathering last of light, she owns no dimension against the lambent and undimensional grass. But she is there, solid amid the abstract earth. He walks lightly upon it, returning, treading lightly that frail inextricable canopy of the subterrene slumber—Helen and the bishops, the kings and the graceless seraphim (*H*, 213).

Ike scarcely knows the ground he walks on, much less of its dust as the reduction of disputes "Betwixt damnation and impassioned clay," but of all this Mink has come to apprehend something. Thus Faulkner may allow one Snopes, little ignorant Mink, vengeful murderer by a primitive code, to approach the fringe of such a glorious company, to be judged with compassion under the common law of life as ordeal, endured in representative human terms. Mink, though abandoned, exposed, and blind to much, is no Oedipus, setting out at last alone and august; he has been tricked and betrayed and retaliates according to his convictions, but he is no Hamlet, neither such a gentleman nor so much a doubter, and being not only the lowliest of commoners but with no present faithful friend, certainly not destined to burial with honors. Neither, however, is Mink the statistically monumental, ideologically glamorized common man ground down by villainous capitalism, though he has existed on the economic margin and in no little bitterness of heart about it. He too is simply and impressively one of those whom Hightower elegized, along with Joe Christmas, when he said, "Poor man. Poor mankind" (*LA*, 93).

Mink of *The Mansion* will no doubt be generally recognized as one of Faulkner's major characterizations; the particular nature of the achievement deserves notice, as one facet of Faulkner's technique. It is something for Mink to have promoted himself into a sense of belonging, if only to the kingdom of the dead, by little but a long stretch of penal servitude bounded by two murders. The point is that just as it took him a lifetime to reach this moment of vision and identification, so by Faulkner's great skill Mink has been seen all along more and more clearly, cumulatively revealed throughout the trilogy, less in his own growth than growing upon the spectator, who is called to a role of insight and empathy. Conversely in the mature Linda of *The Mansion* a more complex character is nevertheless more promptly approximated, through the intuitions of the three who watch and aid, and who read her implicit fate in a web of circumstance stretching out from Jefferson to the fields of Spain. If with Flem's death contrived she emancipates herself from mansion and town, it is into a world to which she is still deafened, so that she still exists in a tragic suspension, a woman prematurely superannuated by a society not good enough for the goodness the innocent fastidious girl of *The Town* had seemed capable of. Mink, appearing more directly in immediate event and in his simple accommodations thereto, is discovered with a comprehension and a pathos gradually deepening. With him, the simple is found subtle; with Linda the complex is given salience. By diverse methods Faulkner rounds out the fictional composition, upon which he throws added lights from respective angles through a trio of ironic commentators who all play the representative human roles of concern and response. It is a protean practice, but it is bound up in terms of two elements envisaged as universals—the ubiquity and persistence of evil, and the innate tendency in many men to resist it, often themselves skeptically and even grotesquely, but with a slight edge, so far, and no disposition yet to give over, though a complete congruity remains out of reach, and consciousness of this as man's fate brings in the eternal notes of melancholy and irony.

While the story is broadly based in the Mink-Flem-Linda-Gavin configuration, it is through Gavin's most searching view and subtler experience that the whole is gathered up. But not until the end, for Gavin as well as the reader, when under Ratliff's comments Linda is recognized as intentional agent of vengeance, and Gavin, having helped secure Mink's release, faces all that he was accessory to. Beyond his collusion, what he must the more lament is the cumulative cost to Linda, in the sacrifice of innocence, gentleness, and serenity, through her involvement with those of mankind who have warped her life. Under that dominating fatality she may seem to be revenging not only her mother against Flem, as Ratliff suggests, but her lost husband against the larger Snopesism of all undue process, including war. Gavin's involvement holds him, also, and he ends, beyond professional rectitude, by carrying to the hiding murderer a first payment from Linda to support him as fugitive. The novel's concluding passage, elegizing Mink's paradoxical progress, a flight into a sense of community as a mortal, has been much and rightly admired, but it is in context, as related to the whole composition, that it is most admirable. It is structurally supported by and reverberantly enhances the immediately preceding episodes in which Linda had pointed out the door for Mink's escape and Gavin had brought him the money, for in these the struggle against evil, with evil-determined weapons, strains every comfortable illusion of peace in one's time, and the tragic will not be summarized in a sudden death alone but appears also in life as ordeal, for Mink, for Linda, and for Gavin too, in the prolonged not-death but deadly trial of the heart which they all, as Faulkner says, endured.

In the perspectives extended by the completion of Faulkner's trilogy, his achievement looms larger than ever as a triumph of realism, through an art drawing on traditional modes—epic concept, dramatic chorus, and fictional penetration of the subjective within a chronicle—yet also an art of unique intent and devices, sounding resonantly its personal tone, disclosing the actual through the grotesque, adumbrating verities by the indirections of irony, and authenticating the humanly representative by provincial instance acutely specified. Genuinely a Southern writer by breeding and commitment, Faulkner has nevertheless always been more than regionalist. It illuminates a range of literary and cultural history in America and also gives some measure of Faulkner's magnitude to note him uncontainable in anything like a New Englander's parochialism or a Westerner's camp isolated in space and time, and to see how far he stands above other contemporary fictionists concerned with American society—the superficial and morbidly rancorous Sinclair Lewis, Dos Passos the thoughtful student but plodding documentarian, Steinbeck keenly observant but of unsteady conscience subject to anarchistic sentimentality. By Faulkner's masculine vitality and tremendous productivity and also by the range of each of his novels he is set above his two most excellent contemporaries in the sheer art of fiction, Katherine Anne Porter and Eudora Welty. One is turned back to *Huckleberry Finn* for something comparable as vision and performance, and in mirroring a regional society Mark Twain had the advantage of a simpler epoch, a picaresque procedure, and an easier containment in a juvenile point of view and in Huck's comparative detachment, reiterated at the end. (This contrasts with young Chick Mallison's involvement in *Intruder in the Dust,* where his dilemma and choice resemble Huck's but foreshadow Charles's permanent adult commitment, and Huck's maturation is surpassed too by Bayard's lengthy progress, in *The Unvanquished*, from child's play to precocious violence to searing renunciation.) The broad stage of Yoknapatawpha County, the full cast of the novels in toto, the crucial conflicts in multiplied instances give an impressive sense of man in society, but without reduction to sociological thesis, and the characters, arrested as of that ghostly aspect Faulkner's art so tellingly captures, are yet seen in their habits as they lived and live, their idiosyncrasies aspects of a reality both personal and abstract, the grotesque an actuality born of stress, the absurd made not only credible but open to ironic confrontation.

It all depends, however, upon immediacy, verisimilitude, singularity, and force of characterization. This, joined to a sustained sense of socio-ethical import and given wide narrative range, enables Faulkner to make a dramatic action of reaction and to represent tentative consciousness, deeply self-aware and even self-beset, as nevertheless primarily responsive to external event and moved to a part in it. In this response judicious reflection, ardent feeling, and active assertion are intricately reciprocal, and bound by a containing mood to represent temperament. With Faulkner's characters the formation of attitude as a process in itself is no mere preliminary to the real story, or something to be disposed of summarily. It does not follow after that American naturalism which allows the narrowest social science to define man for it as a structure of conditioned reflexes and the creature of external determinants, reducing action to that of puppets or pawns, with no logic of motive and indeed no very clear glimpse of the mover's hand. Faulkner rises to a genuine realism which not only documents events and searches motives but celebrates the saving mystery of man's innate urge to postulate values and to react in terms of these evaluations, in resistance to devaluation and in successive, often ironic corrections of his own eccentricities. If Snopesism is object, response to it is subject, and if besides the trio of chief respondents in *The Mansion* two Snopeses figure—Montgomery Ward the remorseful betrayer and Mink the intent avenger— it is so that evolution of attitude precedent to emerging action may be more widely traced, in a realization of man alive, by a scrutiny of "poor man" extended to embrace "poor mankind." Realism, for Faulkner, thus has its roots in what he speaks of as "the human heart and its dilemma."

If Faulkner does not make a set naturalistic pattern the measure for all mankind, neither does he pause too long in the back eddies of a self-examining stream of consciousness. Proceeding from "as a man thinketh, so is he" to the corollary "so acts he," the Faulkner narrative implies that concepts, bred between temperament and circumstance, have consequences, and it is out of the human heart that human behavior proceeds, to be echoed again in consciousness and so to issue realigned as further assertion. Not the least part of Faulkner's achievement is his aesthetic synthesis of motive rising out of reactive process to take overt form, with the action moving to the pulse and breath of attitude deeply grounded and, above all, continuously reconstituted, ever tentative, usually partial and often even eccentric, but always operative. Here would seem to be a crux for Faulkner criticism—to assess adequately his presentation of this existential reality, this sustained sense of being in the process of becoming what it instantly is in terms of a response at once subjective and effective, yet never resting in itself or its result, since it is constituted in a continuum both psychological and external, from which it derives and to which it contributes, becoming the past to create a further present yet still to flow in upon it and be itself modified by modifying. Perhaps more than anything else it is this persuasively fictional representation of action rooted in reaction and returning upon it which makes Faulkner's many-faceted and massive realism so peculiarly impressive.

It is in this aspect, finally, that Faulkner's spectator-interlocutor-interventionists take on greatest importance and an interest beyond their overt doings as reporters and shapers of events. Their performance of those more conventional roles, whether as assessor of the scene or as actor in it, can best be appreciated when the constancy and uniqueness of each one's involvement are recognized, as something both principled and personal, containing in a subjective response that pertinence of issue which is the life of drama. In Yoknapatawpha County its "sole owner and proprietor"[1] has created what is often termed a world, and this is not only because a large miscellaneous troupe of characters have been identified and deployed, it is because witnessing, they are witnessed and witnessed to so intensely. Not a unique accomplishment in modern fiction, it remains a special one, at the very top of this bent, and to overlook it is to devaluate Faulkner. To grant him his due, his work merits in this respect comparison with for instance such a generally acknowledged achievement of highest rank as "Heart of Darkness." The power of that great story, beyond its narrative composition, modulation of pace, palpable imagery, and searching theme, derives from Marlow's presence as more than observant bystander, as one caught up, impinged upon, implicated and all but lost, and emergent not without traumata, his honor paradoxically sustained by concession. It is not primarily Kurtz's story, but Marlow's, whose ordeal in an ultimate confrontation is no less exacting, and the narrative takes its power not just from Marlow's continuous presence, but from the complexity and severity of his personal involvement, which Conrad conveys

[1] *Absalom, Absalom!,* appended map of Yoknapatawpha County, p. 384.

line upon line. So it is with Faulkner's comparable characters.

The spectator-interlocutors are all conspicuously important, but standing even above Ratliff or Charles Mallison in this light, Gavin Stevens becomes the primary and pivotal figure. Indeed, essentially he is the trilogy's most dramatic character, in that through him is given the closest view of a most ardent engagement with reality. This, for him, is based in and begins with a dialogue of self and soul, so to speak, or what he more fancifully thinks of as "that quantity, entity with which he had spent a great deal of his life talking or rather having to listen to (his skeleton perhaps, which would outlast the rest of him by a few months or years—and without doubt would spend that time moralising at him while he would be helpless to answer back)" (*M*, 378). Turned outward, such responsiveness remains the same, tentative, scrupulous, and indefatigably idealistic, as in Ratliff's hypothesizing about McCarron's victory over five waylaying swains in the courting of Eula Varner—"I think I prefer it to happened all at once. Or that aint quite right neither. I think what I prefer is, that them five timorous local stallions actively brought about the very exact thing they finally nerved their desperation up to try to prevent" (*M*, 119). And Ratliff, though amused, is not merely amusing himself; he like Gavin is trying to understand, so that further judgment may proceed soundly and principle be validated, and consequently in some of that Gavin-phraseology he has picked up he can say later, "I mean, I prefer that even that citadel was still maiden right up to this moment. No: what I mean is, I wont have nothing else for the simple dramatic verities except that ever thing happened right there that night and all at once" (*M*, 122), and this because "there aint no acceptable degrees between what has got to be right and what jest can possibly be" (*M*, 124). As elsewhere and in other matters too, here

Ratliff like Gavin is Aristotelian, conceiving what ought to be according to probability and necessity—the latter in its large romantic sense, as well—pushing on from fact to hope, earnestly ironic, searching reality for intimations of ideality.

As creative artist Faulkner too finds the rightful in "what jest can possibly be." Interpretively, like Charles he ponders what "would or anyway should" be (*M*, 205), in a "perusal" like Gavin's of life "in ring by concentric ring" (*T*, 316). Only as instrument of such subtle and comprehensively searching aims can Faulkner's narrative techniques, together with their extraordinary implementation by style, be rightly viewed. His work is not necessarily interdict simply because it is the opposite of the simple-declarative all aboveboard first-to-last mode derived by exaggeration from Hemingway. A more telling distinction is from that stream of consciousness writing which gathers into a tremulous pool mirroring a temperament's preoccupation with its own image. Busy as a Faulkner character often is with his private thoughts and feelings, these are always vis-à-vis a situation, in a real and sustained involvement. In this existential reality, while memory may haunt, even pervasively, it is reconstituted by how it bears upon and qualifies the present, and that new configuration becomes the ground of further intention and action. Whenever in more conventional stream-of-consciousness fiction a character's remembering not only grows haunting but often halts event and takes over, mortgaging present moment to repossess the past, this too, in its way, can be true to life, but to a lesser aspect of it, and it is significant that much of such writing is concerned with persons in solitude or at leisure. Faulkner usually sees life more widely, and pictures men and women in their commonalty and workaday engagement, but responsive consciousness is never minimized, and continuously gives to decision and overt action their embodying and validating third dimension. Faulkner's most representative characters ponder a lot, but not abstractly, in detachment; what they meditate analytically is motive and behavior, others' and their own, in the context of real encounter, and to determine immediate principled reaction, in championship of the humanely preferable.

It pertains to the arresting interest of Faulkner's works that he has taken as a chief function of realism such a dramatizing of responsive man—literally reflective, not a remote theorizer and not the introspective taker of his own pulse, but ardently answerable in a human situation. Confrontation and engagement, as essences of drama, are treated with full regard for their interaction, and for the values that can be imparted to the engagement only by the realized significance of the confrontation. Faulkner's fiction accords full treatment both to the diversity and clash of men in society and to the continuum of individual response, "quick, forgetive, apprehensive," and at once intuitive and judicious, in the way of organic mind. Such a representation may lose the name of action as some name it, but not its essence. Nothing is more vital than that process of scrutiny and evaluation Faulkner traces in all his works, but especially and at greatest length in the trilogy *Snopes*, and when this process is rounded out with relevant emotion and intent response it becomes decisive, not just for the character himself but in its dramatically precipitating influence.

And in both senses of the phrase, not a moment is lost. What the mind inclines to the hand attempts to perform, what the hand encounters the mind seeks to know, and all with utmost expedition, considering the sheer variety and intricacy of the material. Within the terms of Faulkner's broad conceptions and intensive techniques the story is always at full tilt; even the sentences themselves, crowded and extended though they sometimes are, have a constant momentum supplied by emergence of the new or the newly viewed yet always apropos. While Faulkner is a vigorous inventor of elaborate plots, which he furnishes forth with munificent detail, nothing is a surer index of his powerful and original artistry than the way it progressively carries along so much of recapitulation. Neither allusion to preceding events nor review of whole episodes is obstructive or even retarding, but augmentative, as to plot, character, and theme. Never idly digressive nor elaborative for its own sake, Faulkner's is a faithful and pointed realism in which even simplest happenings are shown dimensioned and faceted, their every aspect a relative one, illustrating the complexion of experience, representing onward existence as searchingly as possible within the limits of a fiction.

Motion is the word, but with Faulkner it requires discerning and comprehensive definition. While all fiction and all drama evolve a continuity and depend upon it, its design and manipulation are matters of particular device, sometimes a most telling factor in the artistic effect. Faulkner has said that "all any story is" is "man in the ageless, eternal struggles . . . shown for a moment in a dramatic instant of the furious motion of being alive" (*FU*, 239). Similarly he defined the fictional subject as "people in motion, alive, in the conflict of the heart with itself or with its fellows or with its environment" (*FU*, 251). The movement in Faulkner's fiction, however, is anything but a straight procedure in time, minute by minute, or a simple progression, as in a denotative system. The "furious motion" of characters "alive" involves recollection and expectation; recollection (as the instance may suggest) draws upon anything from the insistent past; simultaneously expectation compounds (out of the immediate experience and its affinities for anything precedent) an apprehension, a fear, a hope, or a desire, becoming an intention, all this "a moment in a dramatic instant," the point of very being.

The personal past, recurrently present, makes recollection as natural as breathing, evincing a serious and normally functional intelligence of whatever grade, and taking on too an aspect of piety, as to self and surroundings consequentially acknowledged. Extended, this becomes the sense for history, backbone of the civil and the humane; but the source is in any man's consciousness, and this reality is something the fictionist must be responsible to. Faulkner has explained his attempt in this regard:

There is no such thing really as was because the past is. It is a part of every man, every woman, and every moment. All of his and her ancestry, background, is all a part of himself and herself at any moment. And so a man, a character in a story at any moment of action is not just himself as he is then, he is all that made him, and the long sentence is an attempt to get his past and possibly his future into the instant in which he does something (*FU*, 84).

In general Faulkner's sentence structures have powerfully advanced this purpose, and much of the quibbling about them seems to disclose a failure to read fully what the fiction is saying.

Sentences, however, are but elementary units in the novel's structure; the gathering up proceeds over wider and wider areas, until all the novel's detail becomes reverberant, temporally and relevantly. It is in this spirit that Gavin Stevens, rejecting the poet's lament that "Fancy passed me by and nothing will remain," asserts the continuity of being and the conservation of the matter of experience, and declares:

Nothing cannot remain anywhere since nothing is vacuum and vacuum is paradox and unbearable and we will have none of it even if we would, the damned-fool poet's Nothing steadily and perennially full of perennially new and perennially renewed anguishes for me to measure my stature against whenever I need reassure myself that I also am Motion (*T*, 135).

Such being man's existence, the capture of that quiddity has been the desire of many modern fictionists. They have gone about it in different ways, though, and not always with success. Here is one of the points at which the originality and extent of Faulkner's achievement is most definitely marked with genius, and this because he has grappled with the experiential in all its complexity and yet has contained it within a dramatic storytelling.

Some such quest is attributed by Lawrence Durrell to his novelist-character Pursewarden, among whose "Consequential Data" is found this note on n-dimensional fiction:

The narrative momentum forward is countersprung by references backwards in time. . . . A marriage of past and present with the flying multiplicity of the future racing towards one.[2]

The proposition may indicate two levels; the first sentence could mean only the manipulation of continuity for the enhancement of plot, chiefly as suspense, an old enough trick, but the second statement centers the fictional representation subjectively in the actors. This is more specially defined in Durrell's *Clea* as

The continuous present, which is the real history of that collective anecdote, the human mind; when the past is dead and the future represented only by desire and fear, what of that adventive moment which can't be measured, can't be dismissed?[3]

If experience thus shown is common, it is augustly so, and an identification with it becomes a profound knowledge,

[2] *Justine* (New York: Dutton, 1957), p. 248.
[3] *Clea* (London: Faber and Faber, 1960), p. 14.

merging life and art, the immediate graced with relevance and rectified in perspective. That which Faulkner proffers he feels, having called himself "a man in motion who also happens to be a writer" (*FU*, viii). He shows it in his characters not just incidentally but by making it his subject; and in providing readers with the sense of it, he impregnates his fiction with a central and recurrent human reality, "perennially new and perennially renewed."

Obviously such realities, in their complexity, diversity, and transience, are not fully communicable. Of all which is thus veiled and largely submerged Faulkner makes the reader the more aware by dramatizing the struggle to apprehend it, and this effect too he has brought to high pitch in the trilogy *Snopes*. A character's scrutiny of another character or a situation can show where to look and can at least trace the limits of discernment, and this method creates that speculative mode which fosters intuition without depreciating mystery. Charles, for instance, hearing his mother and his Uncle Gavin conversing at cross purposes while the three look into a store window, sees them talking "simply at the two empty reflections in the plate glass" and finds it like

maybe two written thoughts sealed forever at the same moment into two bottles and cast into the sea to float and drift with the tides and the currents on to the cooling world's end itself, still immune, still intact and inviolate, still ideas and still true and even still facts whether any eye ever saw them again or any other idea ever responded and sprang to them, to be elated or validated or grieved (*T*, 199).

In this way the grotesque, even extending sometimes beyond the perceived object to a fanciful analogy, at least locates and silhouettes the largely indefinable, caught up out of the flow of other lives into the living motion of a reflective mind.

As a phase of Faulkner's conceptual and stylistic practice

the grotesque, so conspicuously and powerfully employed, is doubly more than fad or flourish, in that it not only can define the norm in terms of the aberration but is made the special means of encompassing that perennial reality currently termed the existential absurd. If fictional tradition is discovered here, and if connections with Dickens are remarked as to a sociological focus, and with Conrad in his ethical probings, Faulkner's further specialization should be noted too. In both Dickens and Conrad grotesqueness, which a careless view might dismiss as exuberance if not affectation, may be seen as the studied aesthetic means of a serious art, responsible to interactive character and circumstance, in terms of thematic value judgments. With Faulkner, however, the grotesque is more subjectively implicated, as part of his characters' "furious motion of being alive," and that impetuous multi-responsive involvement contributes to the distortion, thus serving a realism not of definition but of experience itself and its dramatizing. Faulkner's specialization becomes even plainer in contrast with a more immediate predecessor in the tradition, Sherwood Anderson, who made the grotesque a fictional theme and pictured in his Winesburg eccentrics not only the distorting effects of obsession but some of its roots in societal and personal inadequacies and in the difficulty of communication. Appearing in separate sketches, their paths not often crossing despite the smallness of the community, these Winesburg characters are isolate, their griefs secret, and their crises largely solitary, and George Willard as spectator, entering less into the actions than do Faulkner's comparable folk, remains primarily the reporter of episodes who despite his empathies is detached enough to escape at last, from community itself. This marks in Anderson a formally determined and positively limited theme, made more apparent by a sometimes intrusive insistence. In Faulkner what lies deeper than any theme is temperament—his characters' and his own almost pained sensitivity to the specter-shadows frequently cast by men's most purposeful efforts, so that the more explicit an intention (whether Flem's, Mink's, Linda's, or Gavin's, for instance) the greater its liability to exaggeration, until the discrepant swells into what may be the ominous or even the terrifying.

It is thus that Faulkner's grotesquerie goes beyond caricature, which (as typified by the political cartoon wielding the well-ground ax) is seldom disinterestedly comprehensive and almost never compassionate. The element of pathos differentiates Faulkner's grotesque also from pure comedy with its surface satire and unemotive wit. Yet while the grotesque throughout Faulkner's work is with proper artistry more a matter of dominant creative mood than a formalized thesis, it must be recognized too upon its large conceptual grounds and not mistaken for expedient single effect or self-indulgent mannerism. It is best seen as some aspect of the truth writ very large, like the magnified shadow of a common object, somewhat distorted but mainly a massive correspondence, gaining force by an immense looming simplification. (Again the aesthetic resemblance to some modern painting is evident.) Every leading character in the Snopes saga casts such a moving silhouette, and so does every main trend in their intentions, whether Flem's animal acquisitiveness or Gavin's quixotic intervention or whatever else between. Indeed Faulkner seldom brings even the most minor character into view without some touch of the grotesque, often to a humorous extreme, but not so much for nominal identification as to give an immediate sense of unique human entity, solitary in its concerned consciousness of self and externality, with its intent assertion as of the moment a prey to its own exaggerations, and yet warily adaptive, no matter how quaint and even risible its tactics.

In his great and indeed noble seriousness Faulkner can be funny too, and knows it, and thinks enough of it to have given Phil Stone credit for doing "half the laughing."[4] This is no anomaly, since the comic as Faulkner sees it is a facet, not a separable aspect, of total experience, which also includes the tragic. Faulkner's is a comprehensive realism in which his interlocutors, like Marlow as seen in Conrad's *Chance*, are given to "the habit of pursuing general ideas in a peculiar manner, between jest and earnest" (23). The peculiarity is distinctive, that combination of detachment and concern which marks the essentially civilized man, a disinterestedness at once magnanimous, modest, and acute. Alert to discrepancy, such a mind recognizes extremes, whether as comic accident or tragic fate, and knows too their tendency to merge. Faulkner has said that "there's not too fine a distinction between humor and tragedy . . . even tragedy is in a way walking a tightrope . . . between the bizarre and the terrible" (*FU*, 39). This concept he apparently derives not from critical dicta but from human nature itself, "people, with their aspirations and their struggles and the bizarre, the comic, and the tragic conditions they get themselves into" (*FU*, 177). As to aspirations, since he finds these epitomized for instance among Old Testament characters in two types, those "trying to get something for nothing" or those trying "to be braver than they are" (*FU*, 167), it is with the latter that grotesqueness appears as quixotism, bringing "humor and tragedy" close together. To the suggestion that Gavin Stevens is a bit like Don Quixote, Faulkner, an admiring reader of Cervantes, assented and then declared the quixotic "a constant sad and funny picture too" but "a very fine qual-

---

[4] *The Town,* dedication.

ity in human nature," one which he hoped "will always endure," though "comical and a little sad" (*FU*, 141).

Thus elements merge in Faulkner's vision; reality's contradictions, though irreconcilable, are contained in the work of art, and are offered opportune to the reader's grasp and empathy. The grotesque itself thus becomes a special stimulus to humane perception. Here again a resemblance may be seen between Faulkner's protagonists and Conrad's Marlow, who in *Chance* (Part I, "The Damsel"; Part II, "The Knight"), telling the tale of the quixotic Captain Roderick Anthony's concern for the distressed Flora de Barral, and remarking that "people laugh at absurdities that are very far from being comic" and do so, according to some philosophers and psychologists, "from a sense of superiority" (283), then concludes that

simplicity, honesty, warmth of feeling, delicacy of heart and of conduct, self-confidence, magnanimity are laughed at, because the presence of these traits in a man's character often puts him into difficult, cruel or absurd situations (283–84).

Gavin's quixotism, Ratliff's wryness, Charles's fanciful realism, and all the vagaries of Snopesism caught up together in Faulkner's composition thus await the reader in a grotesqueness that is much more than the farcical, as also it differs from the classically tragic. While conforming to neither of such types, the Faulknerian work sounds every tone from the ludicrous to the melancholy, and in this comprehensive art the grotesque, given ironic ambivalence, is indeed a catalyzer, contributing to organic structure and sustained modulation.

One plainly recurrent but always freshly manifested quality, Faulkner's very hallmark, is what might be called opalescence, that immediate conceptual merging and fluid aesthetic mingling of the diverse and even the antithetical, achieving in fiction, in terms of motion, a genuine, sustained tragicomic mode. In the fourth part of *The Hamlet* is a clear example, the pages describing the sale of wild horses, stubborn Henry Armstid's brutality to his wife and his injury in the stampede, and Varner's coming to tend him with his veterinary's bag; there is the rich surrealistic imagery of the milling horses, the violent humor of mishap sobered by serious accident, the shadow of Flem as exploiter falling most sharply upon Mrs. Armstid, Ratliff's wryly amused consciousness of his own discomfiture, and Varner's rustic vulgarity under the moon that beautifully silvers the pear tree where the mockingbird sings, with the injured man's groans eliciting Varner's folk epigram—"Breathing is a sight-draft dated yesterday" (353). Such opalescence is found in *The Mansion* too, if anything more pervasive than in the trilogy's earlier sections, while also less marked, the method refined to a golden mean, the antithetical modes deeply interfused. With Faulkner the comic is not a relaxing interlude to make way for a renewed tensing in pity and terror; it is rather the lighter side of the grotesque, almost a picturesqueness of the absurd, with humor the regulative medium of both judgment and compassion. Thus there are thematically relevant points to all the jests, recurrent irony frames event in the perspective of detachment, and even slapstick episode wears the aura of anarchic folly as its darker abstraction. The opalescent mode, comprising extremes, manifests a supreme artistic synthesis, structure and texture truly composed, because concurrently and correlatively hit upon and evolved by an imagination capable of sustaining a continuously operant interaction between instance and implication. Everything counts, and the parts are not merely relevant, but related, in an intensified dramatic continuum.

A contributive factor is the persistent tone of irony, voiced by the characters in understatement which, paradoxically accelerative, never minimizes but rather frames event in a perspective of detached value judgments. A token of disinterested, concerned responsiveness, this irony is often too made an aspect of human endurance, in a refusal to be overborne by circumstance. Since an attitude of resolute confrontation is in itself an element of literary realism, its maintenance within the story in terms of character and action adds immensely to the total effect, supplementing verisimilitude with dramatic tension. Most centrally, however, the ironic in Faulkner lifts the realistic presentational to the level of the representative in the evolvement of theme. Irony voices the several characters' quietly insistent ethical protests, made the more impersonal by cool laconicism and the more pointed by wit. All this overlies the pity, so broadly extended, and the terror-equivalent, a controlled but severe apprehensiveness, yet in Faulkner's massive over-all composition these elements of the tragic will seem the constant from which the recurrent comedy is thrown back as a shaped echo, dimensioned to what Walter Allen has termed "the grandeur of Faulkner's tragic imagination."[5]

Herein is discoverable a significant modern trend which Faulkner may be seen to have carried to further refinement, in all his work but especially by the aesthetic fusing of massive and miscellaneous substance and by drawing together diverse actions under the focusing lens of a humanistic theme in the trilogy *Snopes*. That the grotesque, under the control of irony, may become the medium of the tragicomic has been increasingly recognized by some criticism. Thomas Mann, in a preface to the German edition of *The Secret Agent* which praised Conrad's "untrammelled objectivity," took occasion to cite the grotesque as modern art's "most genuine style." This he connected with a discarding of "the categories of

[5] *New York Times Book Review,* November 15, 1959.

tragic and comic, or the dramatic classifications, tragedy and comedy."[6] In Erich Auerbach's *Mimesis* that process, traced in examples throughout Western literature's "serious realism," is seen more particularly in a "modern realism in the form it reached in France in the early nineteenth century," an "aesthetic phenomenon, characterized by complete emancipation" from the often-reiterated ancient doctrine of "levels of literary representation."[7] Mann, feeling that "modern art . . . sees life as tragi-comedy," declared that consequently "the grotesque . . . is the only guise in which the sublime may appear." And his statement that "the comic-grotesque" has always been the "strong point" of Anglo-Saxon art prompts a further recognition that the grotesque, no longer restricted to comedy, may embody the tragic as well, as is particularly true with Faulkner. That herein is a profoundly right intention toward a more organic art, and an art more responsible to reality, should be evident. The formula that life is a comedy to those who think, a tragedy to those who feel, would be definitive if there were such human categories, but man both thinks and feels and his thoughts and feelings in their complication may be matters for either laughter or tears and sometimes both. This total reality, comprising extremes and antitheses, strains the individual in his striving for comprehension and admits the liability to distortion, so that the grotesque emerges in dark profile against the illuminating ideal. It becomes the fictionist's task and privilege (which Faulkner constantly embraces) to represent tragicomic reality as a whole, indivisible and irreducible without loss of essence.

In consequence it may become a function of realism to allow certain fictional characters an ironic perception com-

[6] *Past Masters* (New York: Knopf, 1933), pp. 231 ff.
[7] *Mimesis* (Princeton, 1953), especially pp. 554 ff.

parable to the fictionist's own and to that presupposed in
other men of good will and anxious mind. Irony thus employed in fiction can encompass the grotesque with a peculiar
force, by mirroring the mode of the thing confronted, meeting the inordinate in its own terms yet without surrender.
Ratliff repeatedly will pinpoint the outrageous by an extreme
understatement, and Gavin will suggest the scrupulousness
of his evaluations by giving full play to exaggerated fancies,
until their incredibility becomes a foil to the veracious. Irony
can thus be an ideal regulative mode, implying a human
competence without heroics, a conviction principled and
ardent enough to coexist with tentativeness and even skepti-
cism, and a reassuring detachment. By its acceptance of "the
human heart's dilemma" and its engaging with the consequent discrepancies and distortions, irony rises to fortitude,
equalizes judicious perspective and concerned involvement,
and expresses the tragicomic through an organic work of art
that does not minimize the inextricable tangle and ceaseless
flux of life, nor on the other hand deny those configurations
of meaning in vindication of values which men are capable
of conceiving and partially enacting.

Such is Faulkner's vision of reality, and he has made his
rhetoric ample for the aesthetic expression of it. That rhetoric, the total stylistic and narrative strategy, while rooted
in conventions, is in the main even more original than the
vision. In both is the free play of intuition, and the two inter-
permeate as immediate sensibility and conceptual power in
an imagination meriting the supreme epithet, Shakespearian.
Indeed, in one way Faulkner surpasses the Elizabethans and
the fictionists who in their wake have also essayed the tragicomic. He has come closer to comprising the matter whole,
tragicomedy unhyphenated. "This t., called life 1649"—thus
the O.E.D. cites the term, and thus three centuries later

Faulkner has glimpsed a present reality and reviewed it for the reader. Consequently the dense texture, the antithetical stresses, the progressive realignments of past and present, and the structural counterpoint. Hence the opalescent surface, its colors changed with shifting points of view, but its details never extracted from the total reality, its meanings never oversimplified by isolation from their constantly and multifariously qualifying context. To look into the mansion is to look out upon the town and back to the hamlet—and beyond. In *Snopes* the provincial locale becomes cosmic in its tragicomic realism. Moreover, the real presence of the past, its continuous refraction and reconstitution by event, the natural human glance forward and impetus into the future, and the continuum of a remembering, responsive consciousness stretched taut between extremes yet inclusive of humor and sorrow, judgment and compassion, and expressive in its assertions—all this is what Faulkner renders.

The first marvel is the encompassing vision, the sheer conceptual containment. The second and not lesser marvel is its rendition, not by abstraction but by recreation of this reality as known to living breathing men going their ways wryly, with laughter and tears, but onward, under their author's announced belief that "living is motion" and his artistic sense that such motion should be rendered with something of its accumulated thrust, its immediate and transcendent complexity, and its inexorable effective continuation. Faulkner's creations, steadily illuminated by sheer creative genius of the first order, form themselves under this aspect, which if not of eternity at least is of the ideal as Santayana defined it, as "a function of reality." Moving to the pulses of time as a condition of human existence, Faulkner's art is also deeply true to the mind's ranging powers and all that looking before and after which reaps hope and grief and man's acceptance of grief for the sake of hope.